DEDICATION

To Henrietta Cohen Leitner,
the first of many wonderful gifts
I've been given in my life.

As Paul Anka wrote:
"If in death the good Lord is kind,
You'll be the last thing on my mind."

Rest in peace, Mom.

A few words about "bad words"

As most of you know, the language of sports can often be off-color, profane, and coarse – and, of course, hilarious.

The truth is, John and I discussed this at length because we were concerned about possibly offending anyone.

So, rather than risk offending even a small number of readers – including those who spoke the actual words – we decided to include only a few of the "bad words."

Final clincher: Would I want my mom to have read those words in her boy's book?

No.

Your mom? Probably not.

There, I feel better already.

Uncle Teddy

CONTENTS

INTRODUCTION
BILL WALTON

TED LEITNER is one of the most important people in the history of San Diego. Not just in sports, but in every aspect of our lives.

He's been in our living rooms, in our heads, and in our souls, for more than 40 years.

Whether it's Chick Hearn, Vin Scully, Ralph Lawler or Jerry Coleman, Dick Enberg or Ted Leitner, these are the guys who make us believe that our commitment and loyalty to the cause is worth the effort, time, and sacrifice to get to the promised land of tomorrow.

He's one of those rare and different dudes – a spiritual force of nature like few others.

Ted and I have a shared spirit. He's one of those rare and different dudes – a spiritual force of nature like few others.

He's able to communicate hope, joy and optimism, and a positive path forward.

Ted is incredibly creative, radiantly brilliant, and such a quick thinker. Most of his work is unscripted, which awes, amazes and inspires me.

Ted Leitner has always been a man of integrity, credibility, character, values, and standards. He represents the best of the human spirit—always willing to stand up, and do the right thing.

Ted Leitner is very much a spiritual healer. He knows the challenges that we're facing. He knows what we're looking for – often before we realize it ourselves.

Ted has a joyful, upbeat, passionate delivery style that is in-different to any particular event, medium, or the stars above.

He's a purpose-driven story teller – beautifully taking us on unexpected journeys.

We can always count on Ted Leitner – as reliable a per-former as I've ever known.

As convincing, authentic and enthusiastic as Ted always is – he should've started his own religion.

The grind of being Ted Leitner has to be overwhelming. That kind of devotion to your calling takes a brutal toll on your family, friendships, and everything else.

But Ted has always embraced these risks and challenges – constantly willing to share his emotions, frailties, and limita-tions, regularly letting all of us into the depths, recesses and sometime excesses of his heart and soul.

I was there.

On January 18, 2014.

As a privileged member of the faithful audience at San Di-ego's PETCO Park, the day the Padres honored the memory of the recently departed Jerry Coleman.

It was as powerful and emotional as any event I've ever attended. Ted Leitner was the reason why – shepherding us through our times of trouble and devastating loss.

He was our beacon of hope, our shining star then – as he has unwaveringly been, seemingly forever.

I am honored and privileged to be a student and disciple of Ted Leitner. My life has been positively impacted and shaped by Ted Leitner.

I'm a better, smarter, and more reflective person because of my 44 years with Ted Leitner. He is the voice of knowledge, compassion, reason, conscience, and reality. And that's just for starters.

I'm awestruck by Ted Leitner. I miss him and love him more than words can tell.

Teach on, Ted. Lead us. Carry us to a better future.

With eternal and boundless love, gratitude, admiration, respect, and appreciation, I thank you, Ted, for your life.

Which has given me mine.

Shine on, forevermore.

BW

There's nothing like talking into a red-hot microphone.

1

You're an adult, right?

*"I've tried to avoid acting like
an adult as much as possible."*

WHEN THE PADRES' OPENING DAY 2021 came, my son Matthew texted me and asked, "Did you go to the game?"

And I said, "No, no, no."

I knew I wasn't ready for that, and I certainly wasn't ready to go up to the press box as if nothing had changed. I couldn't even think about going up there and not doing the play-by-play. No way.

So, I missed Opening Day on purpose.

A few days later, when I was invited by Padres chairman Peter Seidler to watch the game with him in the Petco Park owner's box, I had lots of mixed feelings and not a little trepidation.

Since early November 2020, when the Padres made the official announcement that I had retired from the booth, I had to keep telling myself that, OK, you were part of the Padres' broadcast for 41 years.

You had a good run, but now it's time to shut up, get on with it, make the transition, and live the rest of your life without doing baseball play-by-play, which I've loved doing all these years.

I've tried, I really have.

Just after the season started, I was talking with Brad Lidge, the former Phillies and Astros closer who's now a host on MLB Radio.

He said, "With all the young talent the Padres have, how come you walked away from the broadcast booth now?"

And I said, "Brad, there's a very good reason for that. And that reason is very simple: I'm really, really stupid."

During spring training and throughout the first months of the 2021 season, I'd have these occasional dreams – nightmares, really – about going up to the press box and sitting down in my regular chair in the broadcast booth, all ready to do that night's game.

Except, when I got there, there wasn't anyone who knew me. It was as if they'd all forgotten me, as if I'd never been there before, that I hadn't done what I did for 41 years.

So, I'd talk myself into waking up from that awful nightmare and I'd be wide awake and really depressed. That's when I'd say to myself, OK, here's the deal, Teddy. You're an adult, right? Why don't you start acting like one?

Of course, I've tried to avoid acting like an adult as much as possible. That's a big part of the reason why I've spent my life talking into a red hot microphone about sports and politics and whatever else came out of my big mouth.

The truth is, I've loved doing what I've been doing ever since I started talking for a living. And it's been quite a ride since I first started doing high school football play-by-play in the Oklahoma outpost known as Cushing.

That's where I first heard one of my favorite opening lines, especially when I'd do those morning sports reports, 7:15 am and 8:15 am, KFMB 760: "A big ol' country howdy to you."

Believe me, I didn't learn *that* growing up in the Bronx and Yonkers, New York, where I spent my so-called "formative years."

⸺⸙⸺

When I was first coming up in the business, starting in Oklahoma City, then in Hartford, and then in Philadelphia, which was definitely *not* the highlight of my career, my favorite play-by-play sports to do were football, basketball, and then baseball, in that order.

But all that changed in early 1980 when my beloved friend and broadcast partner Jerry Coleman was hired by Padres owner Ray Kroc to be the Padres' new manager, which surprised all of us, even Jerry.

After that first season, I came to love doing baseball play-by-play, which is amazing because I was strictly a football and basketball play-by-play guy – no hockey, not ever – until that 1980 season.

After Jerry got fired as manager at the end of that disappointing season, he was promised that he'd go back up to the booth to resume doing play-by-play as the lead voice.

Believe me, it was absolutely wonderful to have him back, and I know Jerry felt much more comfortable watching the game from the booth instead of managing a subpar team of misfits that finished 73–89, dead last in the National League West.

He tried, he really did.

Now, when I think about the past 41 years, I can't help but remember the uproarious laughter Jerry and I shared every day, every game, every year. It's as if we never stopped laughing, on-air, off-air, didn't matter.

What a ride.

All that laughter about so much crazy, silly stuff – like "What'd you *do* today, Jer?" – that we couldn't stop laughing about. Still can't.

When I think about how blessed I've been in my professional life, so blessed and so lucky, let me say that working alongside Jerry Coleman was one of the greatest privileges of my life.

It was just *so* wonderful.

2

Really, really strange

"You don't know me. I'm the guy on Channel 8."

I'VE ALWAYS BELIEVED that you can count on one hand the number of your life's best friends, and Jerry was on that one hand. No one else comes close.

He was more than my broadcasting partner. He was my brother. He was my dad. He was a mentor. Most of all, he was my friend.

When I first came to San Diego to work at Channel 8, listening to him do the Padres games was like an out-of-body experience for me. Growing up in New York, I had watched him play since the early 1950s when he was with the Yankees and I was just a little kid.

At the time, I didn't know enough baseball to realize that, hey, this guy can play, but I did know the name Jerry Coleman. He wasn't as big of a name as, say, Phil Rizzuto or Billy Martin or Yogi Berra or, of course, Jerry's roommate, Mickey Mantle, but he was big part of the Yankees' dynasty, that's for sure.

So, I got here in 1978 and started doing my Channel 8 stuff as the new guy in town that nobody knew.

At night, after doing the 5:30 and 6:30 sports, I turned on the Padres' radio broadcasts and I'd hear this guy named Jerry Coleman doing play-by-play. I remember thinking, "Hmm, that's got to be the same Jerry Coleman who played for the Yankees. I don't believe it."

And I let it go at that, as a coincidence.

Then in July of that year, after Billy Martin got fired by George Steinbrenner, the first of five times, I decided to call Jerry at his home in La Jolla and I said, "You don't know me, but I'm the guy on Channel 8."

He said, "Oh, yeah, I watch you a lot. You sound like a New Yorker. What can I do for you?"

I said, "Well, since you're a former teammate of Billy's, I'd like to know if I could bring a crew over to your house, if possible, because I don't want to make you come to the studio. Then we could shoot something about Billy Martin getting fired. Could we do that?"

"Oh, sure, no problem."

Of course, he said yes, because as I found out later, Jerry said yes to everything ... absolutely everything.

So, I went over there, and even though we had never met before, he was unbelievably welcoming to me and our camera crew. Of course, he was that way with everyone.

Jerry was the first to teach me that lesson, that our job is to give back to the community that's supporting us as broadcasters.

I had that reinforced when Larry Lucchino was the Padres' CEO and he'd always tell his management people in no uncertain terms, "Our job is to say yes!"

Looking around his den as we set up the shot – and it was film then, not videotape – I couldn't believe my eyes because I didn't see anything, I mean, *nothing*, to indicate that he had ever played for the Yankees of my youth.

No trophies. No photos. No bats. No gloves. No balls. No plaques. Not even a Yankees cap.

Then I started to look for anything about his military career. After all, he was the only major-leaguer to serve in two wars, World War II and the Korean Conflict, both times interrupting his pro baseball career as a Marine.

Nope, nothing. Not even a Marine Corps insignia of some sort.

It was like he had never played in the majors and had never fought for his country in two wars. I thought to myself, "Isn't that amazing?" Then I thought, no, it's more than amazing. That's really, really strange.

For some reason, maybe out of respect, I didn't bring it up at the time.

Later, of course, we discussed it, always at my prodding, many, many times both on and off the air.

Over the years, of course, I came to understand the reason he never liked to talk about himself or his amazing careers. It was perfectly clear that he must've had his ego surgically removed at birth. There could be no other explanation. Mine, by the way, remains intact.

For Jerry, for as long as I knew him, and I wish our friendship could've gone on forever, it wasn't about what happened "back then" that mattered the most to him, it was, hey, what's next.

That was Jerry's philosophy of life, and he did that every day throughout his life, for as long as he lived. And even at 89, he died much too young.

What a wonderful, wonderful man. I learned so much from him. I can't tell you how much I miss him, still.

But I'll try, probably through tears.

When Jerry Coleman was the Padres' manager in 1980, our interviews had moments of levity for both of us. Think my shirt collars are wide enough?

3

Like he was a horse

"Man, I've never seen anyone do that."

On the Padres' charter flights back in the "old days," the manager and coaches were usually seated in first class, and Jerry and I sat in coach, each of us in the first-row aisle bulkhead seats, sitting directly across from each other.

It was me on the right side, him on the left.

When Jerry wasn't sound asleep, which wasn't often, we'd talk across the aisle. But as soon as that plane left the ground, he would fall deep asleep. Then he'd somehow wake up just at the exact moment we'd be landing, a skill that always amazed me.

Back in the early 1980s, along with Dave Campbell, Jerry and I were in Montreal taking the subway from the hotel downtown to the Big O, Olympic Stadium, one of the all-time worst baseball stadiums in history, by the way.

The seats on our subway train were all taken, so we had to hold onto the hanging straps, just like in the subways of New

York, and we're making stop after stop. That's when Dave elbowed me and pointed his chin toward Jerry.

Jerry was absolutely, totally fast asleep, standing up, like he was a horse!

As the train started up again, Jerry's head was bobbing up and down to the train's start-up rhythm. Dave and I couldn't believe our eyes. Then he stopped nodding and was totally asleep.

Of course, Dave and I were no strangers to traveling, but I looked at him and said, "Man, I've never seen anyone do that."

But that was Jerry.

Another time, and Jerry told me this himself, it was in the early 1990s when he was still doing CBS Radio's weekly Game of the Week, which was carried nationally on Sunday nights throughout the season.

That meant Jerry would finish doing the Padres' Saturday night game, then race to the airport and catch a late flight somewhere, wherever he happened to be assigned that week.

Sometimes, they'd make him take a cross-country flight to the East Coast, which didn't really matter to Jerry because, as I say, he could sleep anywhere.

At the time, by contrast, I was the prototypical white-knuckle flyer, so I couldn't sleep a wink on most flights.

Anyway, he's retelling this story and this is what happened: First, he flew from San Diego to LAX via a commuter flight, and then he's on his way to Chicago.

Being Jerry, he tells me, "I guess I fell asleep while we were taxiing, and then suddenly I woke up and we were landing, so I thought everything was fine."

Little did he know that while he'd been asleep, the pilot had made several rather important announcements. Turns out that plane had encountered a bird strike and it had caused a cracked windshield.

So, an hour on their way to Chicago, they made the decision to turn around and return to LA, since that would be quicker and safer.

Jerry, of course, assumes that since they've just landed that he's now in Chicago. He gets up, takes his overhead luggage and walks into the terminal.

They've already told the passengers when he was sleeping that they have to exit the plane, gather in a big group, and wait for a customer service representative.

There's no way to fix this windshield in any short length of time. They're all told, don't worry, we'll get you to Chicago as soon as possible.

Meanwhile, Jerry missed all that because he had walked off the plane, without paying much attention to what was going on. When he got to the lobby, he looked around and thought, "This looks familiar. What's going on?"

As usual, he started walking and walking. If you're familiar with O'Hare, you know you're directed downstairs to a long tunnel, which sort of looks like the long basement at LAX, especially if you're not paying attention.

He's looking at the monitor trying to find the carousel number for his bag, and he can't figure out why it's taking so long. He still has no idea where he is.

He's walking along and suddenly thinks to himself, "Hey, this ain't Chicago. Where am I?"

Finally, it occurred to him that, "I'm in Los Angeles. This is LAX." Then he went back upstairs and got in line to catch the next flight to Chicago.

That's the kind of hilarious stuff that went on with Jerry, all the time.

After Jerry told me that story, I said, "Well, I can't say I'm all that surprised, Jer. Don't forget, Dave and I saw you sleeping standing up like a horse in Montreal that one time."

Instead of taking offense, though none was intended because it was just good-natured teasing, Jerry launched into another one of his "Where am I?" adventures.

"Oh, I can beat that," he began. "One time, I was on a mission in Korea, and we had blackout conditions and no lights, no nothing, no radio communication unless it was an emergency.

"I've got my wingman on my right, wingman on my left, and all of a sudden they go, Uh-oh! Seems that I had fallen asleep in the cockpit. *In the cockpit*, during a life-and-death air attack against our enemy."

Talk about relaxed!

I just shook my head in utter amazement, not only that something like that had happened. But also that this American hero had absolutely no reticence in telling that story about himself.

Like I say, that was Jerry.

If you knew him, you knew there was no one else like him.

He was like a shark. You know how they say a shark will die if it stops swimming? That was Jerry. He was always moving forward, never looking back, always in a hurry to get somewhere.

So, in every situation when we were on the road, like coming out of LAX or out of Dodger Stadium with all that traffic, there'd be a cop there with his hand up and Jerry would say to the cabbie, "Go! Go! Go! Go!"

"Jerry, the cop's right there."

"Go around him! Go around him!"

"He's got his hand up, as in STOP."

"I don't care!"

That's just the way he was, in the military and during his playing days and as a broadcaster.

It was a case of "That's my mission, I gotta do it." And he was like that even for what should've been a leisurely drive in and out of a ballpark.

Hearing him retell those stories, I would laugh and laugh and laugh.

Like me but even worse, Jerry had trouble with all this tech stuff like smart phones and iPads and so forth.

In the early 2000s, Nextel gave each member of the broadcast team new flip phones, which were the latest thing. They were ones that had the little "ping" for a text, a longer "ping" for an email and a regular ring for a phone call.

The tones all sounded somewhat similar – especially if you were Jerry.

I'd be driving a rent-a-car and he'd be in the passenger seat, and he'd get a text that went "ping."

And he'd flip up his phone.

"Hello? Hello?"

"Jer. Jer. That's a text. I've got the same phone as you. That's not a phone call, it's a text."

"Oh, OK."

Or, he'd say, "I can't find my phone."

"All right, I'll call it and you answer."

I'd call his number and you'd hear the ring tone on his phone, which happened to be on the floor of the back seat.

"Now, you hear that ring?" I'd say, knowing he didn't know the difference.

"*That's* the phone ring. I'm calling you from my phone, like an old-fashioned phone call. That's not the text ring. So, when it's the longer ring, go ahead and answer it."

Of course, I was teasing him, pretending that I knew so much more than he did about those smart phones that had just come into our lives. But, believe me, I was no techie. Not then, not now.

I always used to tell my later broadcast partner, Jesse Agler, "You know, I can't understand all these hi-tech devices. The only thing I'm able to do is turn 'em on and off, and I even screw that up."

Now that I have grandkids, they know much more about these things than I do.

When it comes to knowing how to use all this techie stuff, I've got to admit that I've *become* Jerry, which really isn't so bad.

4

A couple of crazy stories

"Well, you gotta expose yourself."

FOR ME, THE MOST POPULAR on-air bit in the history of our Padres broadcasts was when I'd ask Jerry, "What'd you do today, Jer?"

Believe it or not, that bit had its origins back to the 1980s, after I'd seen an interview with the comedian Elayne Boosler, who at the time was dating Andy Kaufmann, the manic comic who sadly died too soon, in 1984.

She said she'd do her stand-up routine wherever she happened to be, and sometimes Andy would be in the audience. When there was a slight lull, he would yell out, "Hey, Elayne, what'd you do today?"

She knew it was Andy Kaufmann and she'd laugh and then tell a couple of crazy stories about what she did that day.

Well, a lot of years went by before I came up with the idea of asking Jerry the same question during the broadcast when things got a little slow.

I was certain that it'd be a hit with listeners – for one thing, his stories always made me laugh – for one very simple reason.

People loved Jerry, and I knew they'd get a kick out of hearing his stories.

Of course, even though Jerry wasn't necessarily trying to be funny, his stories turned out to be hilarious, especially since they were all true.

One time we were in Chicago, where it's impossible to get a cab outside Wrigley Field after the game. I mean, there's a thousand cabbies waiting, but you've really got to be aggressive or else you're out of luck and left behind.

Even though I'm a Type A personality – big surprise, right? – I've never been very good at hailing cabs on the street corner, even in New York, where it's mano-a-mano.

But for some reason, Jerry, who was the most polite, considerate man I've ever known or been around, was very good at it.

So, during the Cubs series the next day, I asked him on the air – in a variation on the "What'd you do today, Jer?" theme – why he was so good at getting cabs when I couldn't get a sniff.

"How'd you get that first cab?" I asked, innocently, not having any idea what he was about to say.

"Well," came his reply, "you gotta expose yourself."

"What?"

"You gotta get out there and show 'em," he said, digging a deeper hole. "You gotta run out there, you know what I mean?" – and, of course, by now he realized where I was coming from, the double entendre of what he had said.

Back then, of course, we could slip in a few double entendres here and there. Now, whenever that happens, it's best to simply hand in your resignation letter to the company, whatever the company happens to be. Times have definitely changed.

Trying to dig him a deeper hole, I asked him, mock incredulous, "What do you mean, you gotta expose yourself?"

He knew I was giving him a straight line, like the old Burns & Allen comedy bit, going way back.

Great example: On the old George Burns & Gracie Allen TV show, someone asked Gracie, "On your vacation, did you go by plane or boat?"

And Gracie replied, "How do I know? George bought the tickets."

In fact, I'd call him Gracie sometimes, just because we both got a kick out of it.

"You gotta *expose* yourself?" I repeated for emphasis.

"No, not *that*," came his reply. "You know what I mean. You gotta go out there and get right in front of the cab, go right out in the street and ignore all the people who are yelling and screaming and cursing at you. Just get in the cab and go."

By that time, I'd turned off my mic and started laughing.

When the Colorado Rockies first got started in 1993, we stayed at the Grand Hyatt in downtown Denver, which was a high-end hotel.

A few times, however, when that one was booked, we stayed at the Embassy Suites downtown, which was also located near the ballpark.

Again, not knowing what to expect, I asked Jerry, "What'd you do today, Jer?"

"Well, you know, I got lost," he told our listeners. "I walk every morning because the doctor told me I should walk more, so that's what I do."

And he was right, his cholesterol was way too high. Not so much the triglycerides, but his serum cholesterol was way over 300. His doctor had put him on a walking program, and he'd walk every morning, sometimes for miles.

He continued: "I walked and walked and then I realized I didn't know where I was. So, instead of turning around, I walked and walked and walked some more, hoping to go in the right direction."

And he said, "Downtown Denver is really confusing, you know."

"Well, no, it's not."

Unfazed, he continued: "Finally, I went up to a cop and told him I was with the San Diego Padres and that we were scheduled to play a game here against the Rockies. But that I was lost and I couldn't find my hotel."

"So, the cop asked me where I was staying."

"And I told him I wasn't sure, but that I thought it was called NBC Suites."

As Jerry continued telling the story, he said the cop scratched his head underneath his cap and told him, "Well, I don't know about any NBC Suites."

Pause.

"Do you think it could be Embassy Suites?"

"Yeah, could be, could be."

"Well, in that case, it's down there, and make a left, and then make a right, and that's Embassy Suites."

To me, that's as good or better than any Jerry Coleman story because it was just pure Jerry. Guileless, with just the right comic twist.

Very few people would tell that kind of story about themselves, but Jerry didn't mind because he had, as I say, absolutely no ego. At least, he knew how to put his ego aside.

I happen to know he truly enjoyed his role in "What'd you do today, Jer?" because he told me so. He knew it was our little comedy bit, part of our daily give-and-take repartee. For the record, I wasn't making fun of him or in any way trying to embarrass or disrespect him.

Because, believe me, I would want to die before I would do that.

———❧———

When Sandy Alderson took over as the Padres' CEO, he took me to lunch and said, "We're in a pennant race and you're asking Jerry, 'What'd you do today?' He's talking about taking his dog for a walk. Not good."

I explained that it had been part of the broadcast for years and listeners loved it. It was only about 60 seconds or so out of a three-hour broadcast.

Earlier in the season, I'd had a run-in with Sandy, whom I considered one of the most brilliant baseball men I'd been around. So, I wanted to keep the peace.

He had taken issue with my comment, on-air, after a Padres fan threw a plastic syringe at Barry Bonds.

I said, "I don't care if they have Syringe Night the next time the Giants are back at Petco, and they throw 40,000 syringes at Bonds."

Not good.

Sandy was pissed.

And that was the end of "What'd you do today, Jer?"

I stopped doing it – until early in 2009 when Sandy left the Padres.

That's a behind-the-scenes story that's never been told before.

WE'LL BE RIGHT BACK AFTER THESE WORDS

During the past few years, I've had many people ask me, "Hey, why don't you write a book and put some of your favorite stories in it?"

Stories? You want stories?

Here you go...

PART 1

"A good landing is a landing you can walk away from."

I'll concede that the Mountain West isn't the greatest basketball conference, but there's no doubt that it's the toughest *travel* conference in the country.

There's no comparison.

Getting to Laramie and Fort Collins and Colorado Springs and Logan can be a real pain, not just because of the different altitudes and lack of direct flights, but because of the weather.

In the wintertime, it's brutal.

For example, a few years ago, when the Aztecs were going to Laramie to play Wyoming in basketball, they had chartered a 30-seat private jet that had no bathroom.

Let me repeat: No bathroom.

Psychologically, as a passenger, you have to sit there and think, no, I'm not going to think about it.

"Would you like a drink, sir?"

"Uh, no."

As he usually did, Coach Steve Fisher was sitting on the aisle in the first row, right behind the pilots, who didn't have a door, just a curtain.

It was late at night and the weather was just awful, snowing like crazy with strong winds, which made things difficult – like for landing.

So, the pilot decided to circle above St. George, Utah to wait out the storm for a safer landing – for at least an hour.

Did I mention there was no bathroom?

Where Coach Fisher was, he was close enough to hear one pilot calmly say to the other, "We're running out of fuel. If we stay up here too long, we might not be able to make it."

So, we made an emergency landing in St. George and 30 guys made a mad dash to the men's room.

It's like the old fighter pilots like Jerry Coleman used to say, "A good landing is a landing you can walk away from."

And then run to the bathroom.

We had at least one more unnerving experience – lots more, really – a few years ago on another trip, this time to Logan, Utah.

Again, the Aztecs chartered a 30-seater and we landed in freezing conditions. Because the airport didn't have any hangers, the pilots had to leave the plane outside, unprotected.

After the game, when we arrived at the airport for our flight to San Diego, we could see that the plane was absolutely covered in ice.

We tracked down the clerk who ran the charter flights and asked how long it would take to de-ice the plane.

With a straight face, he said, "Our de-icing equipment is the sun. And the forecast says it'll be here tomorrow."

Sharing a moment with fierce ex-Charger Hank Bauer, the greatest special teams player I've ever seen.

5

An Oklahoma drawl

"I just didn't think it was the right thing to do."

ANOTHER TIME, WE HAPPENED TO BE in Denver again and I asked Jerry my usual, "What'd you do today, Jer?"

And he said, to my utter amazement: "I went to see the Mick. He's signing autographs down at the convention center at a baseball card show."

Silence.

Then I couldn't help myself. I didn't get mad, because we never had an argument or even a cross word between us in all those years, which is amazing in itself.

But I'll admit that I was more than a little irked – and *very* disappointed.

"Jer? Jer? Let me get this straight. You know that Mickey Mantle was – still is – my idol, my hero, right? I've told you how my friends and I tried to walk like him. We talked like him. We had a batting stance like him. We wanted to *be* Mickey Mantle."

Most baseball fans know that the great Bob Costas,

wherever he goes, keeps a prized Mickey Mantle baseball card in his wallet. Beyond the obvious, his irrefutable reasoning has always been that everyone should keep a religious artifact on their person at all times.

Playing ball in the Bronx and then in Yonkers, we all ran the way Mickey ran, even to the point of slowing down slightly because of his bad knees when he'd come around third in a home run trot.

All that stuff.

As Billy Crystal put it in his eulogy to Mantle, he even affected an Oklahoma drawl at his Bar Mitzvah, trying to sound like Mantle on that day.

I said to Jerry: "Let me get this straight. You mean, you went to see Mickey Mantle and you didn't invite me? I know he was your roommate and that you didn't want a third wheel tagging along. But I just can't believe you didn't ask me to join you."

"Ah, well," Jerry replied, "I guess I just didn't think it was the right thing to do. It was just for a few minutes and I didn't want to bug him."

And that's really the way he thought because he had played with and against so many of the game's all-time greats, all those great Yankees, and all those Hall of Famers. He respected their privacy.

Simply put, he didn't want to bug Mickey by bringing someone Mickey didn't know.

It was very similar to how they treated each other as friends and teammates.

When the Yankees were home, Mickey would pick up Jerry at his home in Ridgewood, New Jersey, to take him to the game.

Mickey was always on time, but one time Jerry waited and waited, so he thought Mickey must've been caught in traffic.

But when Jerry decided to look out the window, there was Mickey sitting in his car, waiting for Jerry to come outside.

Finally, Jerry went out to the car and said, "Hey, Rooms, how come you didn't honk the horn and let me know you were here?"

Mantle simply said, "I would never disturb your family like that."

That's the respect they had for each other.

———— ∞ ————

Jerry went on to tell me, "You know, it cost me $25 to get in."

Meaning that Jerry Coleman, Mickey Mantle's former roommate – Jerry used to say that he didn't room with Mickey, he roomed with Mickey's suitcase – had to *pay* to talk to him for a few minutes.

"Jerry, all you had to say was, 'Please tell Mickey that Jerry Coleman is here to see him.'"

"I know, I know," he said. "But you know me, I'm not gonna do that. I'm just not."

"Well, you could've told the guy, 'He's my former roommate and a team member of the Yankees.' I'm sure he would've let you in.'"

"No, no, no."

As it turned out, Jerry gladly paid his $25 and he went up to say hi to Mickey, who was busy signing everything in sight.

At that moment, Mickey saw him and shouted, "Hey, Jerry Coleman! What're you doing here?"

Then, as Jerry tells the story, he mock-complained to Mickey that he had to pay to get in.

"What'd you pay?"

"$25."

"Well, if you wanted me to autograph that picture, it would've cost you $35."

Sitting with my broadcast partner and The Mick would've been one of the highlights of my career.

But it didn't happen.

That was the "What'd you do today, Jerry?" story for that night's game.

The truth is, I did meet Mantle one time, at the Quail Creek Country Club in Oklahoma City when I was doing TV sports there back in the early 1970s.

Someone said to me, "Ted, this is Mickey Mantle."

And I felt like saying, "Really? Is *that* who this is?"

But I just said, "Of course I know who Mickey Mantle is. He was my idol. Great to meet you, Mickey."

I shook his hand and that was that.

My Oklahoma State broadcasting professor, Bob Lacy, who became my mentor and a good friend, told me about a play-by-play opening with the National Hockey League's St. Louis Blues.

Bob had gotten a call from his friend Jack Buck, the Cardinals' legendary play-by-play voice, and Bob told them about me, saying I should at least be considered. Bob gave me Jack's number and said I'd be a fool not to call him, which I did.

Problem was, I'd never done a hockey game – not at any level – in my life. As a kid, I'd been to a few Rangers games at Madison Square Garden and enjoyed those, but I wasn't much of a hockey fan.

My voice trembling, I said, "Hello, Mr. Buck, I know Professor Lacy talked to you and I really appreciate that. But I've only done football and basketball, just nickel-and-dime stuff, plus a few Oklahoma and Oklahoma State football and basketball games on the campus stations.

"So, believe me, I'm no nowhere near qualified to do the NHL. But I just wanted to say hello and tell you how much I admire your work."

Needless to say, I didn't get the job, not even a phone call from the Blues.

Some 15 years or so later, the Padres were in St. Louis against the Cardinals in the old Busch Stadium and Jerry introduced me to Jack Buck in the press box dining room.

I told him that story, and he said, sure, he remembered our phone call. Whether he did or not, I wasn't sure, but the fact that Jack Buck now knew my name was good enough for me.

After that, whenever we'd go to St. Louis, Jerry and I would be sure to get together with Jack, to talk baseball, swap stories and jab each other.

There was the time when Mark Grant of the Padres' broadcast crew was eating in the press box with Jack, who was giving him a hard time about his major-league career, which included six stops along with the Padres.

"You know, Mark, you could've been much better if you had that one pitch."

"What pitch is that, Jack?"

"A strike."

Taking a break with Jerry Coleman in the radio booth. At that moment, there's no other place I'd rather be than talking baseball with Jerry.

6

As if nothing had happened

"Come on up, we'd love to talk to you off the air."

Did I tell you that my partner had trouble remembering names?

We were on the field at Qualcomm Stadium and Jerry was casually chatting before the game with Juan Marichal, the former Giants pitcher who was one of the game's great competitors in the 1960s and early '70s.

Jerry says to me, "You've met Juan, right?"

"No, I haven't."

"Juan, this is Ted Leitner, my broadcast partner."

Then Jerry did what he always did when he was talking to any former major-league star. He'd say, "Hey, why don't you come up and do the third inning?"

He didn't mean just do an interview in the third inning. He meant, take over, do the actual play-by-play. He always did that, though he didn't really mean it.

I'd always say to Jerry, "You know, one of these days someone's gonna take you up on that, and we're gonna have some not-so-great play-by-play. So, maybe you should just say, "Come on up to the booth, we'd love to talk to you."

As things turned out, Juan Marichal came up to the booth just before the third inning. Seeing him standing behind me, I stood up and handed him my headset and microphone, and he proceeded to sit down next to Jerry.

Jerry looked over at him, and noticed that I wasn't there, but he continued doing play-by-play as if nothing had happened.

Then he said, "Hey, we've got a great guest up here in the booth. He's a very recognizable guy, one of the greatest pitchers of all time. How you doing?"

Except I can tell that Jerry doesn't remember his name. He has no idea.

Juan says, "Jerry, I'm doing great," and he starts talking about whatever product he'd been promoting.

While Juan was answering the first question, Jerry clicked off his audio box, took off his headset, then leaned back to me and said, "Who the heck *is* this?" Except he used a much stronger word.

I got a bit closer to Jerry, so Juan wouldn't hear us and I whispered, "Juan Marichal."

"Oh, OK."

It turned out that Marichal didn't really expect to do play-by-play, which was a relief, but he and Jerry chatted for a few minutes when the game resumed.

That sort of stuff happened all the time. We had a ball.

We were in Chicago and for some reason, Moose Skowron, the former Yankees first baseman who was one of Jerry's favorite teammates, was standing next to the batting cage few hours before the game.

Since he was alone for a moment, I introduced myself and said to him, "You know, Jerry's always putting himself down. But he could really play this game, right?"

Skowron looked at me straight in the eye and said, "Hey, Jerry could turn the double-play as well as [the Pirates' Bill] Mazeroski. He was really quick, not a fast runner, but he had really quick hands and footwork."

On a roll, Moose went on: "He'd turn double-plays using just the heel of his glove. That ball would be in and out of his glove like nobody's business. And he could hit behind a runner. He could bunt when we needed a bunt.

"Let me tell you, Jerry Coleman was a terrific player and a *great* teammate."

That's what everyone said about Jerry when I'd ask them about his playing career. I was always looking to get that kind of "inside intelligence" from guys he played with and against, to get them to talk about how good Jerry was. Because they knew.

He was a *very* good major-league baseball player. That's what they all told me.

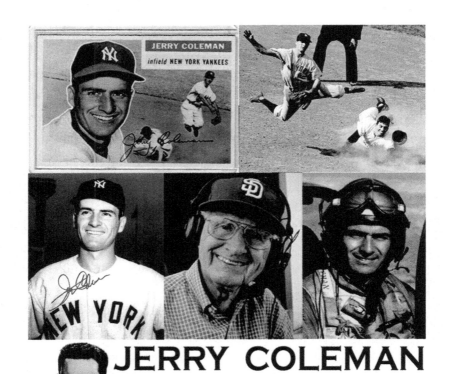

JERRY COLEMAN
1924 - 2014

We salute you, Colonel Coleman.

7

It's not a nickname

"You don't have to die to be a hero."

At the unveiling of Jerry's statue outside Petco Park in 2012 when I was the MC, I said, "You know, a lot of our listeners, until the first Gulf War of the early 1990s, didn't fully realize why we all called him Colonel.

"They must've thought it was a nickname, like Colonel Sanders."

I went on, "Trust me, it's not like Colonel Sanders. It's not a nickname. He was a Lieutenant Colonel in the United States Marine Corps, and the only major-league baseball player to leave the sport twice to engage in combat for his country."

That's the same Jerry Coleman who when we were in Milwaukee, the scoreboard posted a between-innings quiz asking which major-league baseball player left baseball twice to fight for his country.

The multiple-choice answers were Bob Feller, Joe DiMaggio, Yogi Berra and Jerry Coleman.

I turned to Jerry and said, "Look at the scoreboard. What's

the answer to that quiz?" He silently read it and said, "I think it's DiMaggio."

And I said, "No, it's you!"

That was Colonel Jerry Coleman.

This remarkable man was a United States Marine Corps pilot who flew a total of 120 missions in two wars and was awarded two Distinguished Flying Crosses, 13 Air Medals and three Navy Citations.

In fact, every year, the Marine Corps honors a staff non-commissioned officer (NCO) with the Jerry Coleman Award, to recognize "outstanding leadership both on duty and in the civilian community, along with unyielding support for the Marine Corps and the United States of America."

That was Jerry Coleman.

Then and now, he deserves our eternal respect and gratitude, which is quite a contrast to the 1960s and 1970s when our brave American soldiers came back from Vietnam and they were given no respect, no parades, no recognition.

I'm old enough to remember how some of them were spit upon, physically accosted and called "baby killers," as if they were responsible for the unspeakable horrors of that war.

Finally, after the first Gulf War in the early 1990s, our country started to get its priorities right and we began to treat our troops as what they are, courageous warriors who defend our way of life. Young and old. Male and female. And they should be treated with the utmost respect.

That was what Lt. Col. Gerald (Jerry) Francis Coleman meant to me.

When I say Jerry had no ego, you can trust me.

Years ago, someone sent me a picture from Jerry Coleman Day, when he returned from the Korean War and the Yankees held a ceremony for him at jam-packed Yankee Stadium.

The picture shows Jerry at home plate with Mel Allen, the Voice of the Yankees, as MC, and a man in a full-dress Navy uniform.

I looked at it closely and thought to myself, "That's Admiral Bull Halsey, one of the great heroes of all time in the United States Navy."

And it was.

I said to Jerry, "Admiral Halsey was at Jerry Coleman Day? And you didn't tell me?"

"Yeah, he was. Why would I tell you?"

And when the Padres unveiled the statue of Jerry, the one that's outside Petco Park, Admiral Halsey's granddaughter was there representing the family, to honor my partner.

You might think that because we spent so much of our lives together that we must've had lots of verbal scuffles and disagreements.

The truth is, Jerry and I were like an old, happily-married couple, in a marriage of mutual friendship. It wasn't only that we *never* had a fight, or anything close to an argument, it was that we never, and I mean never, had a cross word between us, not one.

Let me add this: As a truly committed heterosexual, if I'd known that Jerry and I would get along so well, as opposed to my marriages, I would've married *him*!

After a game, for example, we never had either of us say, "What did you say that for?" Or, "When you mentioned so and so, why did you say that?"

The only topic that got him riled up was when I'd try to get him to talk about his war record.

"Don't talk about me like I'm some military hero – because I'm not," he'd say. "The only heroes are the ones that didn't come back alive. Nobody else was a hero."

That was the only slight difference of opinion we ever had.

I would say to him, first off-the-air, then on-air: "Jerry, listen to me. Because you and your mates did their job so well, you saved the lives of many of your brothers."

"In my definition, that makes you a hero. You don't have to die to be a hero. You did your job, which you say was just your job, but it wasn't *just* a job. It was a job defending our country."

And he'd come back to me with: "I'm telling you, I don't want you to mention that stuff on the air because I don't think I'm a hero or anything special."

So I told him, "OK, fine, I'll do it when you're not here."

And that's what I did, when he'd step out of the broadcast booth for an inning.

During WWII, Jerry was flying a reconnaissance mission off one of the Japanese islands in the Pacific.

This was an area where we later learned that Japanese captors were executing our soldiers and flyers and then cutting out and eating their hearts as part of a "spirit warrior" ritual.

If missing GIs were captured, they had a very short lifespan.

On his mission, Jerry told me he saw a flash of light coming from one of the islands. He took his plane down to get a better look and saw these two flyboys using a broken mirror to flash signals that they were there.

Jerry called in the PBY aircraft, known as the "flying boat," to come in and try to save these two flyers.

Despite his protests to the contrary, don't tell me that Jerry Coleman wasn't a hero.

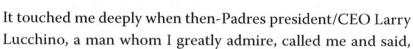

It touched me deeply when then-Padres president/CEO Larry Lucchino, a man whom I greatly admire, called me and said, "You know what? I listened to the broadcast, and I can tell how much respect you have for Jerry."

The fact that Larry, as my boss, would praise me for what I was trying to do made me feel like a million bucks. I was doing it because of my respect for Jerry, who was as great a man as I've ever known.

I thought I was funny, and so did my brothers. But not our grandpa, at least not in this shot.

8

Don't tell your father

"I thought I was the coolest kid around."

WHEN MY KIDS WERE YOUNG, I'd tell them that if they thought they had problems with me, they should feel lucky they hadn't spent two days in our Bronx and Yonkers apartments with that man who was my father.

When I went off to Oklahoma State, he flat-out refused to give me, or my older brothers, for that matter, any spending money for college, so we had to take out student loans and pay them back ourselves, every penny.

As I recall, those loans had an interest rate of about 2 percent, and he wasn't about to spend a dime on my education, which he regarded, in my case, as a waste of my time and his money – if I wanted to be a sportscaster.

I can still remember writing that $77.47 check, over and over, until I paid back every penny.

When my mom, Henrietta Cohen Leitner, sent me letters when I was away at college, she'd put three $10 bills in each letter taken from a bank account that she kept separately and never told my father about.

It was always that kind of thing, when she would tell me, "Don't tell your father." Because we both knew that he'd go into a rage, first against me and then against her.

When I came home for the summer after my freshman year, she bought me my first car, a 1963 maroon Chevy Impala for $1,100. We both told my father that I had paid for it.

Whether he believed us or not, I don't know, but that was my mom's gift to me.

All that summer, driving that car, I thought I was the coolest kid around.

We had bought it from a friend's father, then I drove it from New York back to Stillwater, fighting all kinds of terrible weather.

The worst thing was, the windshield wipers died, which meant that I had to stick my head out the window and try to look through the parts of the windshield that the defroster had cleared, enough to have decent vision to keep driving.

For 26 hours straight.

Come to think of it, almost everything in that car broke down eventually.

Lesson learned? Have a mechanic check out your car, even if it's from your friend's old man.

The main point of the story is that my mother was always very generous to me, even if my father wasn't.

I've tried to have that kind of generosity with my own children, even though – just like my dad – I probably didn't hug them enough. And I know I didn't tell them, "I love you," like I should've and like my father never did to us.

But I sure as heck tried to show them that I loved them in other ways.

In 1968, during my junior year at Oklahoma State, when everyone was worried about getting drafted and being sent to Vietnam, I enlisted in the Army.

I had a drill sergeant, Sgt. King, who was straight from central casting as a prototypical, rock-hard Army drill sergeant.

This was at Fort Polk, Louisiana, not far from the not-so-lovely town of Leesville, which, of course, the soldiers called "DiseaseVille," where they would go on a weekend pass and pick up a "date."

I swear you could light a match against Sgt. King's cheek and he wouldn't feel it. He was tough as nails, which reinforced our thoughts about how lucky we were to have kick-ass guys like Sgt. King, who had fought in Korea and Vietnam.

Whenever he came into our barracks, we'd all be standing at attention in front of our foot lockers, scared to death and just hoping he wouldn't lock eyes with one of us.

The problem was, in a serious setting like that, Sgt. King had an incredible gift for butchering the English language, but we were so scared that we wouldn't dare laugh.

During a foot locker inspection the first week, he said, "You have your socks, your shaving stuff, the stuff you use every day, and the rest of your stuff, the Mussolini items, you put *those* items over here, off to the side."

Standing at attention, we all looked at each other and mouthed, "*Mussolini* items?"

And the guy next to me turned and said, "I think he meant miscellaneous." No kidding.

Right away you'd see one of the guys cover his mouth, trying to stifle a laugh but couldn't.

Then you'd hear a few others do the same thing, up and down the line, with the sounds of guys trying not to laugh so we would, you know, live to train another day.

Then, he'd also caution us about our foot lockers, warning us not to "leave candy and stuff like that, or you're gonna get inserts."

Now, we're really losin' it, and we're looking at each other, mouthing, "*inserts*? He means insects, right?"

———⚭———

When I was on fire-guard duty, I was assigned one night from 2 am to 4 am to make sure no fires broke out, which, thank God, they didn't.

Sgt. King was coming back from DiseaseVille, and I could just smell the alcohol on his breath. He reeked.

To my surprise, he asked me if I wanted a sandwich and then handed me what he called a steak sandwich. Turned out that it was two pieces of white bread and a cooked T-bone steak – with the bone still in it!

I thought, "This guy eats a steak sandwich, then eats the bone like he's a coyote!" I'm tellin' you, this was one tough guy.

After Sgt. King went into his office, I took the sandwich to the trash can, tossed out the bread and then gnawed on the bone like a friggin' animal.

Hey, I was hungry.

That was Sgt. King, the most unintentionally funny guy I'd ever met...until Rickey Henderson.

WE'LL BE RIGHT BACK AFTER THESE WORDS

PART 2

"What ocean do you think it is?"

In 2002, I was with Joan Kroc at the official opening of the Salvation Army Kroc Center on San Diego's University Avenue, which was built from her $80 million gift, one of Joan's many generous donations.

Along with her special guest, Fred Rogers of Mister Rogers' Neighborhood, Joan and I walked into the building.

In the entryway, we passed a framed painting of Joan with her late husband, former Padres owner Ray Kroc, along with their pet dog.

That's when Joan was heard to say, "Well, I liked the dog."

Let's file that under the category of, "There might've been some trouble in paradise.

After a game in which Dave Winfield was called out on a not-close play at home, Ozzie Smith was sitting on his clubhouse stool when Dave walked by.

Ozzie said to him, "Big Black man cannot go as fast as little white baseball."

During a spring training game when the Padres were in Yuma,

John Kruk, one of the all-time funniest Padres, was casually smoking a cigarette in the on-deck circle.

Sitting a few rows away, an older woman said to him, "John, put that out. You're an athlete."

Kruk turned to her and said, "Lady, I ain't no athlete. I'm a baseball player."

When we were on the team bus driving to Chicago's Wrigley Field, Kruk asked Tim Flannery, "Hey, Flan, what ocean is that?"

"What ocean do you *think* it is?"

"Mediterranean?"

"Try Lake Michigan."

The Phillies' Jeff Stone told reporters that he was tired because the team had just arrived after a long flight, and he had a bad case of "jet leg."

Makes sense.

Just about as much sense as when Stone asked a teammate, as they both gazed up at the moon, "Is that the same moon they have back in Arkansas?"

Joe Garagiola, the late St. Louis Cardinals catcher and funny-man who was my Padres TV broadcast partner for two seasons, went very bald before his time.

When I worked with Joe, I told the story on the air that he was driving a rented convertible down I-95 in Florida during spring training.

With the top down, his hair was blowing in the breeze.

"But," I added, "he was much too proud to stop the car and run after it."

Joe liked that line.

When Joe cohosted the *Today Show*, just before he broke for a commercial during a discussion about the Roman Catholic Church, he said, "...and we'll be back with more about the Synod of Bishops in the Vatican."

Unless you're Catholic, you might not know that the Synod of Bishops is an advisory body to the Pope.

Trouble was, thousands of viewers angrily called NBC's switchboard because they thought he had said, "those *sons of bitches* in the Vatican."

That took some explaining.

In a Padres broadcast from the early 1990s, I started out like I was praising Joe when I observed that "Joe Garagiola has forgotten more baseball than I'll ever know."

"And that's the problem. He's forgotten it."

Being Joe, he laughed even harder than I did.

In the early 1980s, the Padres had a first baseman named Broderick Perkins, who added this twist to the classic Willie Nelson/Waylon Jennings song, singing in the clubhouse: "Mamma, don't let your babies grow up to be Kurt Bevacquas."

Mark "Mud" Grant tells the story from 1982 when he was at Single-A Clinton (Iowa) in the Midwest League, and his pitching coach, Steve Cline, came to the mound with a question:

"What was the name of the barber on *The Andy Griffith Show*?"

A bit flustered, Mud answered, "Floyd."

Without another word, Cline turned and walked back to the dugout.

Pretty much the same thing happened to the above-mentioned Joe Garagiola.

It was late in the game, bases loaded, Cardinals up by 1, and Joe's pitcher called him out to talk strategy.

Except the pitcher said, "Hey, Joe, I'm goin' huntin' tomorrow. You know where I can get some shotgun shells around here?"

Joe said he didn't, then turned around and headed back to the plate.

Nothing like a pitcher with his head in the game.

When long-ago Cardinals' pitcher Dizzy Dean was driving with his *Game of the Week* broadcast partner Pee Wee Reese, they passed a gas station.

"Hey, Pee Wee," asked Dizzy, "how do those people know there's oil and gas under that piece of land before they built the station?"

9

The sort of family I wish I had

"They actually talk to each other."

GROWING UP IN THE LEITNER FAMILY, such as it was, we had absolutely no conversation at the dinner table. Not ever.

If any of us dared to say anything, our father would say, "Shut up."

All five of us would sit at the dinner table in total silence while he intently listened to the nightly news on the radio.

When it was time to go to sleep, we three kids would be sent to our bedrooms (one of which we shared) and my parents would unfurl the living-room sofa, which did double-duty until bedtime.

What amazed me most were the actual family conversations that went on at their dinner table. I remember saying to myself, "Wow, listen to this. They actually *talk* to each other."

Same thing when I got to be a teenager. I'd be at a friend's house, and my friend's father would start dinner by asking, "OK, who knows a good joke?" And we'd go around the table.

I learned a few good ones that I would never dare tell at *our* dinner table.

Those families were the sort of family that I wished I had, like the ones I saw on those 1950s black-and-white shows like *Father Knows Best*, *The Donna Reed Show* and *Leave It to Beaver*, featuring the Beaver's mother, played by Barbara Billingsley, who later uttered the classic line in the movie *Airplane*: "Oh, stewardess, I speak jive."

As if those shows reflected anyone's real life. I knew for certain they weren't even close to *my* life.

Our mother, who was known to our friends as Henny, like one of my all-time favorite standup comics, Henny Youngman ("Take my wife, please!"), would get up at 5 in the morning, every morning.

Always in a frantic hurry, she'd make breakfast for our father, make our lunches – usually bologna or cheese sandwiches or leftovers from last night's dinner of roast beef or, my all-time favorite, pot roast – and leave them out on the table in brown paper bags with each of our names on them.

I can still see her handwriting on the bag, TED, though, like everyone else, she called me "Teddy." I don't know why she wrote my name so formally, but that's what she did.

When we were in school, she'd leave a short list of stuff for us to go shopping for, along with a couple dollars or so to get milk and bread at the store down on the corner while she was working.

To get to her job as office manager of a downtown Manhattan millinery firm that made all kinds of hats, she'd first have to take a bus to the subway station, then take the train into

Manhattan. Then she'd walk quite a few more blocks before her work day started.

She would do this routine without complaint every morning and every night, five days a week, like clockwork, with very few variations in her schedule.

Even with both parents working, we weren't rich by any means. But we weren't poor either, at least not for that era or neighborhood.

Still, my father, Murray Leitner, a wine salesman whose territory was the Bronx, refused to spend any money on anything he regarded as extravagant, like, oh, new clothes and shoes.

During school, we ate out at a restaurant maybe once a year when I was growing up. Otherwise, our mother did all the cooking and cleaning, and took care of us kids, all while working full-time.

As far as I know, she never took a day off and never had a sick day.

———— ✖✖✖ ————

During the time I was working in Hartford, our mother's mental and emotional descent into dementia was becoming more apparent, painfully so.

I won't sugar-coat this: After much agonizing, my father decided that we should put her in a mental hospital where she was put through at least one electroshock therapy session. That wasn't a decision my brothers and I made, it was made between her doctors and her husband, our father.

Even today, I try not to think about our mother going through that harrowing experience, which later played out in vivid detail in the 1975 Oscar-winning movie, *One Flew Over the Cuckoo's Nest,* starring Jack Nicholson.

When I saw that movie, I thought to myself, "Oh, my God, *that's* what Mom went through."

I realize that was a long time ago, but it's still very fresh in my mind. Can't shake it, never will.

10

An angry, resentful man

"And I'm wondering what's about to happen."

MY MOTHER, BLESS HER HEART, knew what I liked to eat and she never, ever made me eat anything I didn't like.

That was so important to me because I loved eating – still do – and loved her cooking. Whatever she made, I liked.

I considered it, and her, as my gift.

Though I'm ashamed to say that my mother was the first person I took too much for granted, she never stopped caring for, and about, me.

But – and it's a big but – if ever there was a marriage *not* made in heaven, that was my parents' marriage, if you can call it that. They were so different, just diametrically opposed.

My mother was wonderful.

And my father, to be kind, was *not*.

I can't tell you how truly awful he was because you probably wouldn't believe me. But just imagine an angry, resentful man who would curse his kids and our mother – his wife, a gentle, kind, loving woman who never uttered an angry word in her life.

Just about every day when we were growing up, my father would yell for whatever reasons at my brothers and me using foul language.

There was the time when I was 5 years old and my father was angry at my older brother, Mike, who was 11 at the time.

My father was chasing my brother with a hammer around our small two-bedroom, one-bath apartment.

I couldn't believe my eyes. My brother ran into the bathroom and locked the door behind him. My father started pounding on the door, yelling, "Open this door!"

Eventually, after a few minutes, Mike did open the door and my father hit him a few times, thankfully not with the hammer.

It's been nearly 70 years and I still can't get that ugly scene out of mind. And there were so many more.

As bad as our father was, I'm sure his own father was worse.

And I don't blame him any more than I hope my kids don't blame me for whatever I was like as a father during their childhood, when I was away from my family, way too long and way too often.

For the longest time in my life, it was almost impossible for me to say "I love you" to anyone, especially those whom I really did care for. I was my father's son.

I know I wasn't like my father in a lot of ways, but I should've been able to express the love I have for my boys and my daughter – not to mention my former wives.

But my father had no people skills and no fathering skills whatsoever. Still, I do give him credit. He kept us fed, clothed and kept a roof over our heads.

When I got bigger, between my junior year and senior year of high school, I went from being 5-7 and 160 pounds to 6-0 and 190, I had a size advantage, compared to my father, who was barely 5-9, but was a bully.

When he'd be in the middle of verbally berating my mother about something, who knows what, I'd step between them and say, "I said, that's ENOUGH!"

That was the only way he'd stop. It was awful.

Yes, I fully appreciate the fact that my father did what he could with what he had.

And, I realize that, sadly, many millions of people have similar traumatic childhood experiences, with even worse fathers.

But I'll never get over mine.

Jerry Lewis was my childhood hero, and no one made me laugh more, then or since.

Lo and behold, it turned out he was a Padres fan and wanted to know if he could come up to the booth and sit with me and Jerry.

I think I can arrange that...and I did. Such a talent. I miss him.

11

Don't worry about it

"I didn't know what happens when you do this."

LATE IN MY MOTHER'S LIFE, long after my brothers and I were on our own, I sent her one of those typical Hallmark greeting cards, one of many that I sent her over the years.

On the cover, it said, "Mom, when I was really small, you were all of the world that I knew."

When she opened it, the inscription said, "And what a wonderful world it was."

That's how I felt. And that's what I remember about her.

There were moments I'll never forget because of her acts of kindness to me. Like the time when I was 4 years old and I had to go to the bathroom really bad.

I was wearing my brand-new underwear, which was a step up from the diapers I'd been wearing, and I was darn proud of myself. But now, I was, well, really scared. I didn't know what happened to little kids when this happened. Nature had called.

I remember lying down just outside the bathroom, distraught because I hadn't made it to the toilet in time.

At that moment, I thought to myself, "I'm in such big trouble."

My mom came up the stairs and seeing me, she kneeled down and asked, "So, what's wrong, Teddy?"

"I went in my pants."

She said, "Oh, that's OK, it's not a big deal. Don't worry about it. We'll just change it like we did with your diapers and everything will be fine. Please don't worry about it."

And I thought, "Oh, you Christmas angel, where did you come from?"

Throughout my life, she was always so kind and understanding. As long as I live, I'll never forget that moment. Or her.

Then there was the time when my brothers and I were sitting around the table and our mother sat down and joined us. As usual, we were talking sports and she was just listening, though not really understanding much.

Then we started talking about the Yankees and she just tried to join the conversation by saying, "You know, I've read about that guy with the Yankees, Mickey Man Telly."

She meant Mickey Mantle, of course.

There she was, trying her hardest to relate to her sons and the things we liked.

That touched me so much. Still does.

12

The last thing you remember

"When it was her time to go, I wasn't there for her."

It was October 1978, after I'd been at KFMB for nine months, when my brother Lew called me and said, "I think Mom's had a stroke. The doctor says she didn't, but she's acting like she's had a stroke."

Lew told me that he'd had a conversation with her and that he realized that she thought she was talking to her sister, our Aunt Lilly, not to her son.

That really hurt me because, of course, I wanted to remember her the way she was, not the way she had become at 70, struggling to stay alive.

A few days later, Lew called again and said, "I'm gonna go see her again."

"It's gotten that bad, huh?"

"Yeah, it's bad, but don't you get on a plane. You wouldn't want to see her this way."

Then, he added, "I know how much you love her. But let's not make this the last thing you remember about her."

Given the option of not going, I took the easy way out and said, "OK."

A few days later, on October 12, 1978, Lew called to tell me that she was gone.

It's still a vivid memory for me. The call came in around 10:30 at night, before my scheduled sports segment in the 11 o'clock newscast. I was so distraught that I decided I couldn't go on.

Instead, not wanting to make a scene, I went out to my car and cried my heart out.

The next morning, I flew to Laramie with the Aztecs for their game against Wyoming.

The next morning, I drove to Denver and continued on to New York for my mother's funeral.

I was heartsick for weeks, months, years.

I've never gotten over it.

Sad as it is, that memory reminds me of one of my favorite episodes from *M*A*S*H*, one of my all-time favorite shows.

It's the one where they're all dreaming of their pasts and Colonel Potter drifts back to when he was growing up on a farm. He's riding a horse and he hears someone say, "Sherman, Sherman Potter. Come in."

It's his mother.

That's when Radar abruptly wakes him up to get something signed.

And Colonel Potter says, "Oh, I wish you'd given me one more minute. It's been so long since I've tasted her blueberry muffins."

I was devastated by that scene. Because I loved my mother's cooking.

Since she's been gone, and I realize it's been a long time now, my brothers and I still talk about her pot roast, which we thought was a supreme work of culinary artistry. We loved it *so* much.

I can still hear myself or one of my brothers asking, "Hey, Ma, what's for dinner?"

"Pot roast."

"Oh, yes!"

Just like Sherman Potter with his love of his mother's blueberry muffins, I told my brother, "My God, it's been *so* long since I tasted her pot roast."

There's that famous scene, at least for me, from *Cheers* when Diane's cat has died and she's so upset, beyond consoling.

Sam says, "So what's the big deal?"

And Diane says, "Sam, when I was a kid, that cat was always there for me when I had a bad day. But then when it was her time to go, I wasn't there for her."

I said to myself, "Well, that sounds familiar."

I know I should've gone to see her one last time before she died. I was weak, I was scared and I took the easy way out. There are no excuses.

I should've gotten on the next plane to be by her side, holding her hand as she left this world, just as she was there holding me when I came into the world.

I copped out. I took the easy way out, because my brother was nice enough to give me an excuse for not going.

I'll never forgive myself.

WE'LL BE RIGHT BACK AFTER THESE WORDS

PART 3

"Get outta here. Whadya want?"

In Cincinnati, there was a huge barge on the Ohio River just beyond Three Rivers Stadium, to blast fireworks when the Reds hit a home run.

Pitching for the Cubs that day was former Padres TV broadcaster Rick Sutcliffe, with a former Aztec, Mark Grace, at first.

As Grace tells the story, Sutcliffe had just given up back-to-back home runs to the Reds.

The Cubs' pitching coach, Billy Connors, came out to try and settle down Sutcliffe, who could be fiery in the best of times.

As Connors got to the mound, Sutcliffe snapped, "Get outta here. Whadya want?"

Connors said, "Oh, nothing specific. I just wanted to stall long enough to give that guy on the barge a chance to re-load."

Grace, standing near the mound, said he blew a snot bubble from laughing so hard.

I was with my then-wife when we took the twins to New York as part of a Padres' East Coast road trip.

Once we got to our hotel room, we hastily set up the twins in their cribs and we had a large double bed for ourselves.

As an aside, whenever my kids got to be rambunctious, I'd

tell them to "settle down." I got that from Mr. Gallagher, my 8th grade homeroom teacher who always said that when someone was talking or disrupting class.

After a while, when my then-wife and I assumed they'd be fully asleep, it was time for Teddy to make his move. After all, we hadn't been with each other for 10 days or so.

All of a sudden, breaking the mood of the moment, I heard one of the twins say, "Seckle down, Daddy, seckle down."

———

In 1980, we were on the team bus from Manhattan headed to Queens to play the Mets at Shea Stadium.

Reliever Rollie Fingers, who had a sharp tongue, had blown a save the previous night.

As we passed this huge cemetery, traveling secretary Doc Mattei, who busted everyone's balls, said, "Hey, Fingers, see that cemetery? That's where your arm is buried."

The guys on the bus erupted in laughter.

For once, Rollie had no answer.

That's me in the middle, all dressed up for my junior year photo at Roosevelt High School.

13

Everyone was goin' nuts

"You've got good hands, but you're not fast enough."

W HEN I WAS AT ROOSEVELT HIGH SCHOOL in Yonkers, New York, I played split end and defensive end for the varsity football team, known as the Indians and later changed to the Sharks.

I loved every second of high school football, but trust me, I'm no Allen Iverson because I even liked practice, a lot, even as tough as it was. I'd been waiting to play for Roosevelt since my older brothers Mike and Lew played there.

From about age 10 to 15, all I could think about was, "I can't wait to play for the Indians and wear that red uniform."

A few years before me, Coach Hank Monaco had coached Lew, who played offensive guard and was a fine player. An old-school coach, he had strict rules against swearing, so when I got mad on the field, I had to watch my language, which wasn't easy.

As co-captain, I wanted to set a good example for my teammates. Plus, I didn't want to embarrass myself because if

Coach heard you swear, you'd have to take several bites out of a bar of soap after practice.

I know it's hard to believe, but I'm proud to say that there was not so much as a single soap bubble coming out of this kid's filthy mouth.

———⚉———

Roosevelt was right down the hill from our apartment, and I was in love with that school.

Problem was, I was only 5-6, 160 pounds, which would've been big enough for JV, but I wasn't all that strong, just wiry.

As a result, I didn't make the varsity my junior year. After our last preseason practice, Coach posted a list on the blackboard of the players who had made the final varsity roster.

I walked up to the board, nonchalantly, because I didn't want to show too much emotion. In fact, I put on my helmet so no one would see my facial reaction. I looked and looked and looked for my name, but it wasn't there.

I'm not a religious guy, but I assure you that I was praying that my name would somehow appear on that list. Like the old joke that there's no prayer in public school, but as long as there's math, there'll be plenty of praying.

Well, that was me, praying I had made the varsity.

Finally, I looked down toward the bottom of the list, where it said, "DOWN TO JV," and there was my name.

It was like I'd gotten hit in the face with a bag of nickels. As much as I loved that school and respected my coach, I thought, I ain't gonna be on the team.

I was heartbroken.

As I turned away, still wearing my helmet, I saw Coach Monaco go into his office. I followed him and told him that I'd do my best to get promoted to the varsity.

That's when he told me, "I'm sorry, Teddy, you've got good hands, but you're not fast enough to be a receiver. And you're not big enough to be a defensive end."

A few months after I got cut, the school's athletic director asked me if I'd like to be the public address announcer for Roosevelt's varsity basketball team's home games.

For our games, there'd be a couple thousand cheering fans in that smelly old gym with bad acoustics, and I was thrilled.

I had dreamed about being like my idols, Mel Allen of the Yankees, and Chris Schenkel of CBS who did the New York NFL's Giants in the early 1960s, along with the legendary Marty Glickman, who called the Giants' radio broadcasts later on.

Once, early in my Padres career, I slipped up and used Mel's famous home-run call of "GOING, GOING, GONE!"

This was 1981, when Mel was still hosting the weekly highlight series, *This Week in Baseball*, and that clip of me using Mel's line aired in national syndication.

After the clip was over, he said on-air, "Ted, you and I need to talk." He was kidding, mostly, but that was the last time I used that line, because it wasn't mine.

Since then, I've always been very careful not to "borrow" the catch phrases of other sportscasters. It's like a comic who knowingly steals material from other comics, without giving credit.

Not good.

My junior year, inspired by my new-found prowess as a PA announcer, I started a personal savings fund, my "Tape Recorder Fund" – that's what I wrote on the outside of the jar. I needed just enough to buy a reel-to-reel tape recorder, about $35.

Problem was, though I didn't know it, I "tawked" like I was from the Bronx and I knew I didn't know much of anything except how the Yankees were doing, because I only read the sports page in the New York papers.

That was the full extent of my intellectual curiosity. I knew nothing about anything else.

The other thing I did that impacted my life was more about the power of self-motivation. I knew I still wanted to play varsity football as a senior, so I borrowed my brother Lew's barbells and dumbbells so I could get bigger and stronger.

This was the mid-1960s when "muscle men" like Vic Tanny, Jack LaLanne and Joe Weider were peddling all kinds of powders and pills, some of which actually worked.

Determined to make the team, I lifted weights like a maniac and every day I'd toss down a handful of Bob Hoffman's Hi-Proteen Powder tablets before every meal as if they were vitamins, and I started getting stronger and gaining weight.

Before I knew it, I had gone from 5-6 to 6-feet even, and from 160 to 190 pounds, an incredible natural growth spurt.

Later that summer, I went out for varsity football as a very different Teddy Leitner, and had some amazing early practices that surprised Coach Monaco.

My teammates even voted me co-captain.

Most gratifying of all, my coaches picked me to start both on offense and defense, which was a dream come true.

I had a terrific senior year and made All-City First Team at defensive end.

I would've had a good season on offense, too, but I couldn't see for crap, and for vanity reasons, I didn't want to wear my horn-rimmed glasses, which made me look like a '56 Buick.

Because of football, all of a sudden, I was dating one of the cheerleaders and believe me, it was great. That senior year changed my life.

What I learned was, much like Tony Gwynn worked so hard at his craft – Kawhi Leonard, too – even when they had reached the level of superstardom, you can't just show up.

To be the best, you've got to work hard, you've got to practice, and you've got to want to get better.

So, that's what I did.

───── ❦ ─────

That senior season, my greatest moment had to be when I intercepted a pass in a game against Lincoln High, one of our league rivals.

I swear, I can still see that ball spiraling toward me. I had their receiver covered and I stepped up at the last moment, grabbed the ball and started running toward our goal line.

I'd love to tell you that I scored the winning touchdown, but the truth is that I tripped on the receiver's leg and fell flat on my face. Smooth, huh?

I had dreamed about that wonderful moment for years and it happened right in front of the Roosevelt bleachers. Everyone was goin' nuts, cheering like crazy for me, like I was the greatest player in the history of Roosevelt High School.

I'm not, of course, not even close, but when I got home, I walked into our apartment feeling like I was pretty hot stuff. My mother greeted me with a hug and said, "I heard you had a great game."

My father didn't say a thing. Not a word.

Instead, he slowly walked up and handed me a $5 bill, which really surprised me.

He never said, "Hey, great game, congratulations," or anything like that. Because he couldn't.

But I didn't care, because by that time in my life, I felt nothing but sorry for him. He was an emotional cripple who couldn't bring himself to praise anyone, certainly not his wife or his sons.

With all the psychological pain he caused in our lives, especially to my mom, I just couldn't forgive him.

Like I said, emotionally limited as he was, he did his best to raise us three kids and I'm grateful for that.

14

The tools of ignorance

"But I don't even know where that is."

THE REASON I WENT TO OKLAHOMA STATE was simple: My older brother Mike had gone there, majored in Phys Ed and enjoyed it, and I thought I might be able to play football there.

So I went.

My plan was to try out as a walk-on, but all that changed a few days after classes started when I had a chance meeting with Professor Bob Lacy, chairman of the school's Radio/TV department.

I told him about my interest in doing sports play-by-play and he advised me not to go out for football. Instead, he said, "The guy doing OSU radio now is graduating and if you want the job on the campus station, you've got it" – if I was good enough.

Of course, I said yes, which turned out to be one of the best decisions of my career, because it led to everything that followed.

As a sophomore, I got my first-ever commercial broadcast gig when Professor Lacy asked if I'd like to do Friday night radio for a high school football team, the Cushing High School Tigers, in Cushing, a *very* small country town about 25 miles southeast of Stillwater.

It was a 250-watt radio station whose signal aired only in the daytime, which meant that I had to record my play-by-play on a very bulky reel-to-reel tape recorder. I also had to use a flashlight to see whatever notes I happened to take.

In terms of ability and talent, I'm sure Lindsey Nelson had nothing to worry about.

And Lindsey was certainly making more than my $10 a game.

My games aired on taped delay the next day, heard by several dozen listeners, at least. But I had a great time. And I loved doing play-by-play, even if I had no idea who the players were until a few hours before game time.

First, I'd go to the station and read the newspapers and then go to the high school's stadium, get the printed program even before they started selling them. I'd memorize the names and numbers of the starting quarterbacks, running backs and receivers.

For a non-mathematical brain like mine, I really don't know how I was able to do that. But fortunately, that's how my brain works. Maybe I have a photographic memory, but whatever, it's been a godsend for my play-by-play.

I didn't need a spotter then, and never have.

Doing football, I'm sure I blow a couple of players' IDs, not so much in basketball, but I'm still more comfortable working without a spotter.

Not bragging, just fact. Uncle Teddy is very grateful for that memory skill.

My second paid gig came in my junior year, the fall of 1967, when Professor Lacy asked if I'd be interested in taking a summer radio job in Wellington, a small town in Kansas.

I said, "Sure, but I don't even know where that is."

"It's not that far, maybe an hour, maybe more, from Stillwater," he said. "There's good news and bad news. The good news is, you'll have a play-by-play job. The bad news is, you'll have to spend the entire summer in Wellington, Kansas."

Without knowing exactly what they were offering, I said, "I'll do it."

My last two summers when I was going to OSU, I worked in Wellington, playing Top-40 records as a disc jockey – that's what they were called then – afternoons, 2 to 5, five days a week.

They had what you might call a "mixed" format, trying to appeal to anyone and everyone, but I'd call it nothing but a mess.

They aired something called "The Polka Hour," and another hour dedicated to recordings of the owner's wife, who was an operatic wannabe.

After the opera, we had the farm, fish and market reports, including a mention of the current market rate for ewes, which I didn't know was the word for female sheep.

Being a city guy, I pronounced ewes as "e-wees." Not good.

And on the fish report, I pronounced the species of fish known as "crappies," as it's spelled but not like it *should* be pronounced, as "CROP-ies."

What came out of my mouth was "CRAP-ies."

Made sense to me.

Right after my afternoon Wellington gig at KLEY-AM, I'd hustle off to do play-by-play of Peewee boys' baseball or little girls' softball games around town, either at the local park or wherever the teams played, in and around Wellington.

That was harder than doing high school football, which at least had printed rosters for both teams. All I had was a handwritten list of team rosters, with their names and jersey numbers.

Of course, the little kids weren't very good and made a lot of errors and silly mistakes, but I felt I had to broadcast their games as if I was watching the Yankees against the Red Sox.

For me, it wasn't a case of, "This is Mickey Mouse, get me out of here." All I knew was, it was so much fun to talk into a microphone, doing play-by-play.

Along with an occasional American Legion game in Wichita, which compared to the Peewees really did seem like I was doing major-league play-by-play, I was doing as many as seven games a week and making $100.

I swear, I thought I was rich.

One of my more memorable moments was when the parent of a little kid confronted me for saying that his son, the team catcher, was wearing what I had called "the tools of ignorance," one of the oldest phrases in baseball.

The expression refers to the fact that while catchers are often the smartest players on the field because they call just about every pitch, they're also dumb enough to want to be a catcher – and, in this case, sweat their asses off in the hot summers of rural Kansas.

How hot was it?

My two-year Padres broadcast partner, the late Joe Garagiola, who caught for the St. Louis Cardinals and other major-league teams, once told me that he would lose at least 15 to

20 pounds a game wearing those awful wool uniforms on hot, humid days in St. Louis or elsewhere during the summers of his career.

Now, I ask you, who would want to do that? But this father thought I was bad-mouthing his kid and had called him ignorant.

Talk about ignorant.

My sophomore year, I also worked at Oklahoma State's FM campus station, KOSU-FM, which had a classical music format.

I didn't know anything about classical music and didn't much like it, so I just turned down the studio sound. I'd introduce each recording by reading the LP liner notes word-for-word and then turn off my mic.

One time, the needle got stuck during one of the longer pieces, for like an hour, and all my listeners – assuming we had any – heard that night was, like that old phrase, a broken record. Over and over and over …

A shining moment in my career.

Another one happened when I had the speaker sound "up" in the studio, but I still couldn't hear the music.

Just then, as the station's program director walked into the studio, I turned to him and shouted, "Hey, Larry, I can't hear a thing," meaning the current record being played.

To explain: Wherever you have the studio mic on, it automatically cuts out the speaker so there won't be any feedback. But the dumb ass doing the show didn't know his mic was still on.

Larry never said a word.

He just walked over to me, leaned over my shoulder, reached for my microphone's on-off switch and turned it off. Then he walked out of the studio.

The good news is, it was the campus radio station, so I'm sure no one was listening.

But at least we got respect.

We were at the campus station, after-hours, and we could hear the campus police scanner. The officer in the car out front was radioing into headquarters, saying, "We've got a light on in the Communications Building."

And the dispatcher told him, "Don't worry. It's just those radio-TV squirrels."

Wait, I gave up possibly being a BMOC jock for this?

Yes, and I'm really glad I did.

But I did learn Broadcasting Lesson No. 1: *Always* assume that every microphone in every studio and every press box booth is "hot" – or you will step on your proverbial microphone cord and end your career.

My friend, Tom Brennaman, violated this rule in 2020 and it cost him his job with the Cincinnati Reds and Fox Sports.

The only problem with spending that summer in Wellington was that I wasn't able to go home for the summer. I couldn't help thinking, Mom's getting older. How many times will I see her again?

Here's how much I worried about my mother and her health: When I was in my freshman year, living in one of the student dorms, there was a phone on each floor.

The phone would ring and somebody would answer it, one of the guys on the floor, and they'd call out whoever it was for.

"Someone's on the line for you!" and they'd shout out my

name. Every time, I'd be scared that something had happened to my mom.

That's the way I thought all the time, even during earlier summers when we'd go throughout July and August to what everyone in New York calls the Jersey Shore, where we rented a single room – two beds and cot, a sink, and dresser drawer, but no bathroom.

That was down the hall and shared by the three families, including ours, on the floor of the rooming house.

Back then, I was an occasional sleepwalker and in the middle of the night I'd walk down the hall to go to the bathroom and stop at one of the rooms where a family was sleeping.

Fortunately, we'd known that family for a decade and the mother simply looked up and said firmly, "Teddy, go to bed."

I had no recollection about that until she told me the next morning.

———— ∞ ————

Our mother would work in Manhattan and instead of taking a full two-week vacation, she would work Monday and Tuesday, and then take the train to Bradley Beach, a summer vacation town on the central New Jersey coast.

My brother Lew and I would walk the half-mile or so to the station to meet her, and I'd literally hold my breath, worried that something bad might've happened to her.

As passengers got off the train, I didn't breathe until I saw her getting off the train on the next track over. I was *that* attached to her.

Then the train would pull away and I would see her with the other passengers walking across the track to us by the train station.

It was a wonderful moment that still brings a smile to my

face and a tear to my eye. Some people reach the point where they want to cut the maternal cord, but I didn't.

Still don't.

⸻ ❧ ⸻

When I was a freshman at Oklahoma State, I was asked by Professor Lacy if I wanted to do the Cowboys' football play-by-play on the campus radio station. I jumped at it.

The first game I did was also the first time I'd ever *seen* a college football game in person. After the football season, I also got the gigs for OSU's basketball and baseball games.

In what was one of my early career highlights, my first on-air OSU interview was with Hank Iba, the legendary Oklahoma State basketball coach.

After my first OSU football game, Professor Lacy, who had listened to the Oklahoma State-Arkansas game from Little Rock, critiqued my call.

First, he said, "I have a question, Where is Ar-kan-SAWR?"

Then he said, "Get rid of that New York accent" … pause… "or you ain't gonna get any jobs in this business."

He went on: "You can sound like you're from Oklahoma or somewhere in the Southwest or the Midwest, but sounding like you're from Canarsie Street in Brooklyn ain't gonna cut it."

So, I practiced a lot to sound like I didn't come from where I came from.

15

Tony Gwynn, Part 1

"Oh, I really sounded like my dad then, didn't I?"

WHEN I THINK OF TONY GWYNN, the first thing that comes to mind is that laugh of his. What a great laugh, so infectious, so wonderful.

I don't know anybody who laughed like that. While his son, Tony Jr., doesn't have the exact same laugh, it's darn close.

But when he speaks, he sounds exactly like his father in terms of his speech pattern and intonation. That became clear to me when we did our first game together on the road and Tony Jr. said something that caused me to tear up.

It was right at the end of the final out of an inning and he made a comment that was something his father might've said. Quickly, I looked the other way and went to a commercial break.

While we were in the break, I wiped away a few tears and looked over at him, and he said, "Oh, I really sounded like my dad then, didn't I?"

I said, "Yeah, you sure did."

And I love listening to Tony Jr.

When he was hired by the Padres as the newest addition to our broadcast team, that was a stroke of genius. Some cynics out there might've said that he got the gig because he's Tony's son, and that may be, but he also happens to be terrific.

And like his father, he's one of the best people I've ever known.

———— ∞ ————

When the Padres asked me to MC the Petco Park tribute for Tony, on June 18, 2014, four days after he passed away, I knew I had to do something special.

First, I called a friend and got out-takes from one of Tony's radio commercials, which, of course, included clips of his laugh because he was always laughing.

Then, I cut a part of that laughter, put it on my iPhone, and played it during the tribute.

It was a solemn occasion, but Tony's laugh, that sound of joy and the love he had for the game and his family, his teammates, and for life – that was Tony.

To this day, I still have Tony's laugh and his contact info on my iPhone, just as I do for Dick Enberg, Joe Garagiola, Junior Seau, and Darrel Akerfelds, the Padres' bullpen coach who was such a great guy.

If I need a quick pick-me-up, I'll play Tony's laugh. Works every time.

———— ∞ ————

I'll never forget a flight in 1989 when we had to make a stop in Phoenix because the Padres' 737 charter couldn't go coast-to-coast west-bound without refueling.

While we're waiting on the ground, the Padres brought aboard dozens of hamburgers to feed the troops. I happened to be sitting a couple of rows behind Tony and reliever Mark Davis.

Tony's talking and laughing and not paying attention to his meal. And while he's looking across the aisle, Mark goes over his shoulder and takes the hamburger patty out from between the two buns.

Tony kept eating, even taking a couple of bites as he was talking to guys across the aisle. But by the third bite, he sensed something wasn't right and he blurted out, "Hey, what going on here, man?"

While he could tell that all the guys around him were laughing, he didn't have a clue about what had just happened. Then he picked up the bun of his hamburger, which had a few bites, and finally noticed that the patty was missing.

Then he broke out into the loudest, funniest laugh I've ever heard. It was like music and within seconds, everyone in our section was laughing like crazy.

After a minute or so, we had all calmed down until Tony, who had tears in his eyes from laughing so hard, started laughing again.

That was one of my favorite flights – maybe my all-time favorite – because of that great gag they pulled on Tony.

With Tony Gwynn during a halftime interview on an Aztecs basketball broadcast. We miss you, T ... So much.

16

Watching ping-pong

"You're not gonna make fun of Ted, are you?"

IN THE FINAL REGULAR-SEASON GAME of the 1949 season, it was Jerry Coleman's eighth-inning, bases-loaded "dying swan" double to right field that led to the Yankees' American League title-clinching 5-3 win over the Boston Red Sox.

To Ted Williams, Jerry's hit was nothing more than a lucky bloop, which it may have been. But to Williams, it was also nothing but a fluke, a belief he held until the day he died.

To watch the two of them hurl insults at each other – Ted said it was a "piece of crap" and Jerry said it was "a hard-hit double" – was always a delight.

Whenever they got together at banquets or wherever, Ted would go at Jerry and give him a hard time, like guys do, especially athletes.

Believe me, on those occasions when I happened to be there, it was wonderful to watch.

———— ⚬⚬⚬ ————

Sometime in the 1990s, I was lucky enough to be sitting on the dais between Ted and Jerry at a March of Dimes banquet in San Diego.

It was me, the Giants' broadcaster Jon Miller, the late Phillies' broadcaster Harry Callas, may he rest in peace, plus Ted Williams, and Jerry.

I was between Ted and Jerry.

From the moment Ted and Jerry saw each other that night, the insults between them were flying.

Ted: "Weren't you embarrassed to hit a wounded quail like that in an important situation like that?"

Jerry: "The cover was coming off that thing, it was hit so hard. And I hit it exactly where I wanted to, right behind the runner."

It went on and on. It was like watching ping-pong, back and forth, back and forth.

Ted, of course, wasn't laughing. Jerry was, but not Ted, because he took the game, every game, very seriously.

He simply couldn't could get over that hit, that flimsy hit that had cost the Red Sox the pennant so many decades before. That was his cross to bear, and he never forgave Jerry.

Never.

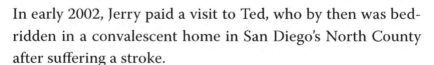

In early 2002, Jerry paid a visit to Ted, who by then was bedridden in a convalescent home in San Diego's North County after suffering a stroke.

Jerry was accompanied by the late Dr. Bobby Brown, who was the Yankees' third baseman and Jerry's teammate in the early 1950s, and then became president of the American League.

Jerry and Bobby grew up in San Francisco of the 1940s, though Jerry went to Lowell High School and Bobby went to Galileo High.

Bobby was one of a kind, and as usual, it was because of Jerry that I was privileged to know him. We're talking about a guy who in the off-seasons of playing for the Yankees was going through medical school, eventually becoming a cardiologist in Fort Worth, Texas.

When he was dating his soon-to-be wife, she was somewhat nervous about taking him home to meet her parents for the first time. She asked Bobby, what should I tell them about you?

Without any ego whatsoever, he said, "Tell your mom that I'm in medical school, studying to be a cardiologist. And tell your dad that I play third base for the Yankees."

How could her parents possibly not like Bobby, a man of integrity and character, who, quite frankly, was just like my partner Jerry Coleman.

Think of it: They had played baseball together as boys on the sandlots of San Francisco and grew to become close teammates on the Yankees and friends for life.

As if that wasn't enough, Yankees catcher Charlie Silvera also grew up with Bobby and Jerry and later was their teammate, with Silvera as backup to the great Yogi Berra.

If anyone needed further confirmation of Bobby Brown's character, in addition to his military service, he was a student at Stanford in 1942 when he witnessed the crash of a Coast Guard plane into San Francisco Bay.

Without a moment's hesitation, he swam out to successfully rescue the survivors.

That was Dr. Bobby Brown.

At the care facility, Ted Williams was in bad shape, recovering from a serious stroke. Jerry and Bobby hoped they might be able to catch him when he was awake enough to share a few laughs and say goodbye.

Jerry and Bobby stood in front of Ted's bed for about 10 minutes, talking to him as if he could hear them, or hoping he did.

All of a sudden, Ted opened his eyes. What he *didn't* say was something like, "Hey, what are you guys doing here? Wow, I must really be in bad shape."

Instead, he looked up at Jerry and said these three words, "That f---in' hit."

Then he closed his eyes and went back to sleep.

That's a direct quote from the great Ted Williams. Not on his deathbed, but close.

Dr. Bobby Brown told that story at Jerry's memorial service. It's a beauty.

Billy Crystal once told Ted Williams that when Billy was a kid, he saw the Red Sox play the Yankees at Yankee Stadium and Ted faced Bobby Shantz, the Yankees' left-hander.

"I was there with my dad and he struck you out," Billy teased Ted. "I couldn't believe it."

Ted said, "Curve ball, down and away."

Not only did Ted remember the game, he remembered the pitch that struck him out.

Great hitters like Ted and Tony Gwynn didn't need all those computerized stats the players have now to tell them how to hit or where to hit. They just hit. And they worked at their craft *all* the time.

And in Ted's case, he also caught record-setting game fish in the Florida Keys and went bird hunting.

Curt Gowdy, the Red Sox voice who later had a long career in TV network sports, talked about the time he went duck hunting with Ted.

Because of his 20/10 vision, Ted could see the ducks coming into view before anyone else could possibly see them.

He'd bark out, "Birds at 11 o'clock," and Gowdy said he'd look and look for 30 seconds, and couldn't see any birds. But Ted could.

That's the kind of eyesight Ted had when he was a fighter pilot in Korea.

Guys like Ted Williams could see the enemy coming at them before the enemy pilots saw them – an incredible advantage when you're fighting a war.

———— ❦ ————

Tony Gwynn had that kind of eyesight, plus exquisite hand-eye coordination and sheer athletic ability.

He could determine the ball rotation, speed, angle, and what kind of pitch was coming at them – all in less than half a second.

And that's what separated guys like Tony and Ted from everyone else.

———— ❦ ————

ESPN's Tim Kurkjian was watching Tony in the batting cage before the Padres' first game of the 1998 World Series against the Yankees at Yankee Stadium.

For some reason, Tony was disgusted and talking to himself, upset that he was fouling off easy pitches he should've been hitting.

As he finished BP, Kurkjian asked him, "Tony, you seem upset. What's wrong?"

"I can't see anymore. I'm old."

"What's your eyesight now?"

"20/10."

Kurkjian said he just shook his head in amazement.

It was such a pleasure on those rare occasions when Tony and Ted got together, as they did one time at Larry Lucchino's house, and talked about the art of hitting.

As Larry's guests, we had to pinch ourselves, thinking how lucky we were to hear these two incredible hitters talk about what they turned into an art form.

WE'LL BE RIGHT BACK AFTER THESE WORDS

PART 4

"I didn't say which way we're praying."

There's no question that Howard Cosell changed sports broadcasting like no one else, for the better, and the stories about him are legendary.

This one happens to be true.

During a *Monday Night Football* telecast in the mid-1970s, ABC Sports producer Don Ohlmeyer said into Cosell's earpiece, "[Patriots head coach Chuck] Fairbanks told me that in this situation, the next play would be a pass to tight end Russ Francis."

"So, Howard, bring that up...*NOW!*" – which he did.

The play resulted in a Patriots touchdown and you can imagine Cosell crowing, as only he could: *"Just like I said! I told you he'd go to Francis!"*

After the game, as the TV crew was in a limo headed for the airport, Cosell bragged to Ohlmeyer: "How'd you like that call, kid?"

Ohlmeyer then caustically reminded Cosell that the tip had come from him: "Do you think that plastic thing in your ear is a radio?"

Frank Gifford, who did MNF's playR by-play for many years, called Cosell when Howard was hospitalized and in failing health.

Gifford told Cosell that he and his wife Kathie Lee were praying for him.

After Cosell thanked him, Gifford said, "Oh, no, Howard, I didn't say which way we're praying."

Famed sports columnist Red Smith had the classic line when Cosell said to him, "Red, I'm my own worst enemy."

And Smith replied: "Not as long as I'm around, Howard."

Later, as Cosell was regaling himself as one of the great sportscasters, he asked Red, "How many great sportscasters do you think there are?"

"One less than you do, Howard."

Frank, the fellow who operates Petco Park's media elevator and is a great guy, gets asked constantly by fans who get on, "How's it going?"

And he always, I mean, *always*, says, "Oh, up and down."

Gets a laugh every time.

Many years ago, I was honored to be memorialized by an Over-the-Line team that chose for its name: "Tourists Go Home – And Take Ted Leitner With You."

One time, in the late '70s, I was in line at a 7-Eleven in Mission Beach, and the customer in front of me turned around and said, "You're Ted Leitner, right?"

After I replied that, yes, I was, he made a reference to a TV special that aired the night before on the execution of Gary Gilmore, whose claim to fame was that he requested the deed be done by firing squad.

He said, "You know that Gary Gilmore guy? That should've been you."

—⚬⚬⚬—

Another time, I walked into a store and a customer thought he recognized me.

Referring to my longtime Channel 8 colleague, he said, "You're Larry Himmel, right?"

I just laughed.

As I walked out, I said to the same guy who was waiting by the door, "By the way, I *am* Larry Himmel."

To which he said: "You wish."

"Son of Sports" was one of many different segments I did on Channel 8 over the years, all with the same general theme – I talked a lot.

17

Tony Gwynn, Part 2

"He could barely walk, which pained me to see."

W<small>HEN</small> I <small>THINK MORE ABOUT</small> T<small>ONY</small> G<small>WYNN</small>, I can't help but wonder how media members and fans reconciled his terrific skills with how his playing weight increased year after year.

The funny thing – not so funny now that he's gone – is that I don't think I ever mentioned anything having to do with his weight on the air.

Maybe I was wrong in not doing that, but whenever it was brought up to him – and I'm talking about in the clubhouse, behind the scenes, not on the air – Tony's response would always be the same.

It was, "Hey, I can play and I can hit and I can defend. Do you think I've lost a step in the outfield? Do you think it's taken away from my throwing accuracy?"

Maybe it was because he was so likable, but when out-of-town sportswriters would bring up the topic of his weight, Tony would give the same answer, that it wasn't a factor in his ability to play at the highest level.

I always think of that scene in the movie *Ray,* one of my favorite movies, where his record-company executives confronted the great Ray Charles because they knew, they're absolutely positive, that he was on drugs.

"Hey, Ray, your slip is starting to show," they'd say.

And he'd say, "Hey, have I ever missed a gig? Do I get it on the first take all the time? If I can still do that, leave me alone."

So, in my defense, I decided not to bring up the topic of Tony's weight because I truly didn't think it was a negative factor in how he was playing – and he played with some incredible injuries.

Like in 1996 when he was suffering from that Achilles injury and bursitis in his right foot.

He played in only 116 games that season, which was amazing in itself, given that I'd see him in terrible pain, out of the public eye, when he was walking around in the clubhouse and hobbling down the aisle on our flights.

After many games, he could barely walk, which pained me to see.

A different injury but the same kind of intense pain also plagued the Padres' Ken Caminiti after he tore his left shoulder rotator cuff early in that 1996 season. He kept on playing and his arm was just hanging down, tight against his body.

The team doctors told me they couldn't believe how messed up his shoulder when they performed surgery at the end of that season, and he was still going out there like the fearless warrior he was.

The same thing was true with Tony. He played hurt, and in pain, and still played really well.

Looking back, all anyone could reasonably say was, "Sure, he can still hit, but his increased weight means he's putting more pressure on his knees," which takes a toll.

I'm sure you could medically make that claim, but to cite one shining example, in 1994, Tony hit .394, one of the highest batting averages in the history of the game.

Was he overweight? No doubt. Could he hit? He had eight batting titles, tied with Honus Wagner and behind only Ty Cobb (11), who both played a very long time ago.

Let's put it this way: Ted Williams famously said that hitting a baseball squarely with a round bat was the most difficult feat in all of sports.

The privilege of watching Anthony Keith Gwynn hit a baseball was a joy to behold.

Caminiti was another dominant force of those Padres teams of the mid- to late-1990s.

When he later revealed in a 2002 *Sports Illustrated* cover story that he'd been on heavy steroids during his playing career, especially with the Padres in his MVP season of 1996, I was as surprised as anyone.

Referring to the article, Padres GM Kevin Towers asked me, "Did you have any idea Cammy was using steroids?"

And I said, "KT, I swear to you that I never thought and I certainly never knew because we don't know much about that drug culture, that steroid culture."

My exchange with KT, who was always honest to a fault, came after he had made a public comment that, "We should have known, and we should have done more," or words to that effect.

But ownership called him in and said, "Hey, don't be making comments like that. That makes it look like we did something wrong and we didn't. We didn't know either."

Looking back on that time, it was obvious that Caminiti's power had greatly increased from his Houston days, along with his foot speed, even his range at third.

When you put those things together, not just with Cammy, but with so many other players, it's clear that we should've known something was different.

But we didn't know crap, so we weren't hiding anything. I can tell you that I never heard anyone say, "Hey, you think Cammy's on juice?"

We *had* heard about Creatine and Human Growth Hormone (HGH), but we didn't know about all the different anabolic steroids and what they could do.

Maybe we should've known more, and dug deeper.

All we had to do was look around to see that the guys who were thought to be steroid users – guys like Barry Bonds, Rafael Palmeiro, Manny Ramirez, and later, Ryan Braun and Alex Rodriguez – didn't pass the eyeball test.

Former Oakland A's slugger Jose Canseco, who definitely didn't pass the eyeball test, once claimed that 85 percent of major leaguers were on steroids. Caminiti's estimate was about 50 percent.

All you had to do was look at some of the players' acne, on their faces, on their backs. Ugly stuff. If you really want to know who does steroids, go into the showers and take a look at their shrunken testicles.

No thanks, I'll pass.

Or take a closer look at their aggravation level, the out-of-control bouts of 'roid rage.

During that era of the late 1990s and early 2000s, there was virtually no standard drug testing in major-league baseball.

But there were a lot of tape-measure home runs by guys who hadn't hit squat before.

To me, that was a very dark era for the sport, and it might be continuing to this day, because steroids work. They make you stronger, quicker, faster – and give you better visual acuity. Who could ask for more?

How 'bout a longer, healthier life after baseball? What's *that* worth?

But fans don't seem to care. It's gotten to the point where too many of us shrug and say, "Why should I care? Go ahead, do what you want to do. It's your body."

Shame on us.

The magic moment when Ted Williams told the photographer (in more colorful language) to take the shot. There was no one like Ted.

18

Taught the right way

"He would rant and rave the rest of the game."

I LOVE THE PHOTO OF ME AND TED WILLIAMS laughing together on the day in 1992 when State Route 56 Parkway in San Diego's Carmel Valley was named in his honor.

A few weeks before the dedication ceremony, Hall of Champions founder Bob Breitbard, who was one of Ted's closest friends from when they went to Hoover High School and until their final days, called to ask if I would serve as MC.

Of course, I said yes.

Then Bob asked me a question that I regarded as slightly insulting, though I'm sure he meant nothing by it. He'd been watching me on Channel 8 and he said, "You're not gonna make fun of Ted, are you?"

I said, "Bobby, just because I do those commentaries and whatever else I do, that doesn't mean I don't respect the game. I do, plus I have the utmost respect for what Ted Williams means to the game and to this city."

I added: "Look, I don't know Ted well enough to risk teasing him. He might take it wrong, so I would never do that. Don't worry, I'm not gonna do anything like that."

In that photo, Ted and I are laughing together like we're old friends, and I'm sure some people will see the picture and wonder, "What're you guys laughing about?"

We were laughing because just before the photographer took the shot, Ted barked, "Come on, get this f---in' thing over with."

That was Ted Williams, in all his F-bomb glory.

We could say for sure that Ted and Jerry had something else in common – though Jerry didn't verbalize it in the profane way that Williams did.

Every time a player on either team would screw up – especially if it was the Padres' second baseman, his pet peeve – we'd go to commercial break and he'd be furious.

Jerry always said, if you're trying to make all the plays you should make, you're going to make errors. And if you don't want to make errors, don't play. But at least act like you care. And, please, use proper fundamentals.

During a break, he'd go into his rant and rave about how too many of today's players had little to no basic fielding fundamentals, that they had no idea about situational hitting, that they were out of position, that they were terrible base-runners, that sort of thing.

When we'd break for commercial, he'd turn to me and say, his face getting redder, "If that guy ever played for me, I'd bench him and he'd never play for me again."

Trust me, he didn't say it exactly that way. Even I'd be taken aback, so I'd say, "Easy, Jer, easy. It's only a game."

To me, it was fascinating how serious he was about the

integrity of the way the game should be played. I'd try to kid him about it and he'd say, "You know what he's gonna be doing after the game?

"He's gonna walk around the clubhouse with a huge plate of food and he's gonna be laughing it up and having a great time and he just cost his club a run, maybe the game.

"When I played, if I did that, I'd want to find a hole to climb into."

He'd go on: "If I made that stupid of an error, you'd need a psychiatrist to get me out of my locker in Yankee Stadium, I'd be so embarrassed. I wouldn't be able to face my teammates. I mean, all guy had to do was take one more step to the left, but instead he tries to showboat and uses one hand."

And on: "If I'm out there, I'm not doing that backhand stuff. I'm getting right in front of that ball with one more step and then I knock it down and make the play. If I try to backhand it and do an olé, suddenly it's passed me for a hit."

"What happened out there was inexcusable."

That's what riled up Jerry, so much that he'd often refuse to go into the Padres' clubhouse after the game. He just couldn't stand it.

He respected the game so much, like his generation did to an amazing degree, and seeing stupid errors, physical and mental, really got him fired up.

In trying to be fair to today's athletes, Jerry would often contend on-air that he wasn't a "Back When I Played the Game, Everything Was Better" sort of guy.

Instead, he would say, "You know, these athletes are bigger, stronger, faster, quicker than we ever were. They're *way* beyond us."

Then we'd take a commercial break and, because he knew it would crack me up, he'd quickly add, "But some of 'em sure piss me off."

That was the Jerry Coleman few fans heard.

And I loved him for it.

19

Tony Gwynn, Part 3

"You know, Ted, Tony loved you."

I FIRST GOT TO KNOW TONY GWYNN in 1978, when I showed up at one of his first Aztecs basketball practices at San Diego State's Peterson Gym.

I introduced myself and I was surprised when he said he knew who I was. But then again, that's when I was ranting and raving and doing commentaries and pissing off at least half my audience on Channel 8.

As one example of the controversy I stirred up at Channel 8, the kid intern in the mailroom came down to my office in the newsroom, delivering my giant stack of daily mail.

Included was a postcard that had only this simple address: "A-hole, News 8, San Diego, CA."

I happened to see that and said to him, "Hey, how did you know that was for me?"

Slightly embarrassed, he said, "Judging from the rest of your daily mail, I assumed that one was yours."

So, I guess I shouldn't have been surprised that Tony knew who I was – because I was *that* guy.

He was an average-sized 5-foot-11 point guard, notably shy and quiet, and we talked for maybe 30 seconds.

We didn't have another conversation until later that season when his 15-foot jumper from the free-throw line against Texas El Paso at the Sports Arena was the game-winner.

Since he was the obvious choice, I had him as our post-game guest for the first time and, believe me, you wouldn't have known it was the same Tony Gwynn that we came to know and love.

I got nothing from him but what seemed like one- or two-word answers and maybe a three-word answer, and I thought to myself, "Kid, you're killin' me here."

Of course, I didn't say that, but years later I always teased him about it. I'd say, "We're in luck, T, I brought my dental tools today."

"What do you mean?"

"Well, like the time I had to pull teeth when I had you on the Aztecs post-game show."

He'd laugh that laugh of his, and I would just smile.

Tony eventually became our beloved "Mr. Padre" not only because of his hitting prowess – he undoubtedly ranks among the game's greatest hitters – but because he was *the* guy for local and national sportswriters and TV crews.

All you had to do was ask Tony one or two questions, on anything, and he'd fill up your notebook with quotes and give you film, and later, video clips galore. It was amazing how much easier he made all of our jobs.

Even the guys he would at first turn down because he was busy, he'd seek them out later and do 30 minutes until *their* notebooks and tape recorders were filled. He was incredibly, wonderfully, amazingly loquacious, funny, and insightful – with everyone.

I always watched him do interviews with a sense of awe because, no matter what the question, he always seemed to have a smile on his face, the same easy-going manner he had when he first came to town.

Think of it: I first got to know Tony when he was a shy teenager and then as a young man, later as a husband, as a father, as eight-time National League batting champion, and, really, an idol – if you want to use that word, and I do – because he was so talented, so popular and so beloved.

In the Petco Park radio broadcast booth, there's a painting of Jerry and me MC'ing an Opening Day ceremony, adorned in our tuxedos and standing at home plate. There's also a great photo of me, Jerry and the late Kevin Towers.

Then there's a photo of Tony.

After he passed away, I'd be doing play-by-play and I'd often lean back during commercial breaks and think about how much I missed Tony. He was such a huge part of my career, and I was blessed to call him a friend.

It was truly a special occasion in late June 2014, a few days or so after Tony had passed, when Fox Sports San Diego invited me, Dick Enberg, Mark Grant, and Tony's widow, Alicia, to share our memories of Tony.

Early in the show, host Mike Pomeranz asked me a question and I started to give an answer when Alicia gently jumped in and said, "You know, Ted, Tony loved you."

I was so blown away.

I'll never forget that moment. It was just incredible.

The same thing happened to me at the private tribute in Jerry's memory when I spoke as the final speaker.

Just before I was about to go to the dais, Jerry's widow, Maggie, leaned over and said to me, "You know, Ted, Jerry loved you."

Those are moments I will never forget – ever, ever, ever.

Maybe the Padres weren't always competitive, but I got to watch at least four Tony Gwynn at-bats in the "game within the game" and I'd always look forward to seeing him perform his artistry.

When he came up to the plate, Jerry and I knew he was showing us how to really hit, how to carve, how to rake, how to play all aspects of the game. It was a wonderful thing to see, a gift that not a lot of home-team broadcasters get to see over a 20-year span.

But I did.

I got to see one of the top hitters of that entire era, travel with him, see him in the clubhouse, hear that laugh, that wonderful laugh. I can still hear it now.

Tony Gwynn was a huge part of my broadcasting career and every game was a gift.

20

Without relying on a script

"It was either going to work or it wasn't."

I STARTED MY TV CAREER AT THE CBS AFFILIATE, KWTV-TV in Oklahoma City during my year of graduate school at the University of Oklahoma in Norman, which is only 20 miles away.

If you thought I was overpaid in San Diego, you'll probably think I was overpaid in Oklahoma City, where I pulled down all of $7,800 a year.

And I got up to that total only by doing the Sunday-night late newscast for a grand total of $15.

That was my first big-time TV gig, doing weekends and I was sure I'd hit the big time.

From the start, I did my first few shows with only a rough typewritten script and a few scribbled notes. Since I'd already memorized much of what I was going to say, it worked out.

I didn't want to stare constantly at the camera, so I'd occasionally break eye contact and make it look like I was looking at my script, to make it appear more natural.

Before I went on the air, I'd tell the director the numerical order of what film clip was coming up. I'd do the same thing before we'd come back from commercial break.

Of course, they had to be in the correct order. Back then, film clips were racked on a single reel and if they screwed up No. 2, then you weren't getting Nos. 3 and 4. That would be disaster.

Sometimes, the film would break and I'd have to ad-lib while they went through the rest of that film clip, getting the next clip ready. Those were the moments when I'd say, "Please, God, take me now."

Toward the end of my time in Oklahoma City, I started doing my segments without using any written notes at all, just an assortment of mental notes that I'd made in my head.

When that red light went on, I looked straight at the camera and talked in my usual straight-forward, obnoxious delivery, strictly from memory.

It was either going to work or it wasn't.

The fact is, when I was in Oklahoma City, I wasn't really trying to "get" anywhere else.

I was just grateful for the opportunity to be on TV and was hoping to get some radio play-by-play to go along with it.

It could've been in any college town – Stillwater or Norman or Tuscaloosa or Columbus or College Station – anyplace where, if I got lucky, I'd also get to do football and basketball play-by-play, and maybe TV sports.

If I had stayed in Oklahoma City, I would've been totally satisfied with my career choice.

The truth is, I only applied for one other job during my time in Oklahoma and that was to do TV sports, plus play-by-play football and basketball in Lincoln, Nebraska for the University of Nebraska.

But I didn't get the job.

As Garth Brooks wrote years later, "Thank God for unanswered prayers."

Otherwise, I would've frozen my ass off forever.

Instead, five years later, I wound up in San Diego.

WE'LL BE RIGHT BACK
AFTER THESE WORDS

PART 5

"Tell Ross to shoo that fly away."

Alvin Dark, who managed the Padres from midway through the '77 season before he was fired during the next season's spring training, once proclaimed that "they'll put a man on the moon" before Gaylord Perry hits a home run.

Amazingly enough, Perry, a notoriously poor hitter who won the Cy Young Award in 1978 with the Padres, made Dark's prediction come true, but just barely.

A few hours after Neil Armstrong walked on the moon on July 20, 1969, Perry hit his first – and only – major-league home run.

As for Gaylord's spitball artistry, I love what his Padres catcher, Gene Tenace, once said about him:

"Sometimes, I couldn't throw the ball back to him because it was so greasy that it slipped out of my hands," he said. "So, I'd just walk out to the mound and flip it to him."

———— ✿ ————

At the start of that '78 season, which was my first covering the Padres, I did a "live" shot with Gaylord and asked him about the team's chances for the upcoming season.

His line was classic: "You know, this team has a strong bench. The only problem is, it starts every day."

Ol' Gaylord never pulled any punches. Whenever one of

his fielders made an error, he'd put both hands on his hips and give that offending teammate a death stare.

If looks could kill.

When Perry was inducted into the Hall of Fame, one writer described the event this way: "When Ferguson Jenkins was introduced, they played the Canadian national anthem. When it was Rod Carew's turn, they played the Panamanian nation anthem. When Gaylord Perry stepped to the podium, it started to rain."

Perfect.

Every Sunday, and this is probably true for every major-league clubhouse, the Padres provide the players with a huge, industrial-sized box of fresh donuts.

The Padres' Hall of Fame reliever, Trevor Hoffman, who's one of the great pranksters of all time, would take a bite out of every one, then carefully place them back into the box.

Of course, after word got around, nobody wanted any of those donuts. But when a rookie or someone new joined the team, Hoffy would do his thing and the veterans would get a kick out of it.

Later, he changed tactics by licking each donut, so no one could tell whether he had done anything or not.

Needless to say, during Hoffy's marvelous career with the Padres, donuts were not a popular snack.

My good friend, Ross Porter, who would later team with Vin Scully for years on the Dodgers' radio broadcasts, had a similar style to mine when he was also doing TV sports in Oklahoma City.

Much like I did, he'd look directly at the camera and rarely break eye contact.

One day, a fly was in the studio and it kept buzzing around his face. He never shooed it away and never broke eye contact with the camera.

It became a legendary story in Oklahoma City, as hundreds of viewers called the station, urging the switchboard operator to have somebody "tell Ross to shoo that fly away...

"Because it's driving us *CRAZY!*"

21

A perfume-scented letter

"Hey, this must be working."

WHEN I ANNOUNCED THAT I HAD TAKEN THE JOB in Hartford, I still had a couple of months left on my contract before I was to leave the Oklahoma City market.

In my final sportscasts in Oklahoma City, I was determined to put pressure on myself to prepare for the transition to a bigger market.

So, I said, "How 'bout doing the sports without any script at all."

I got with the KWTV news director and told him, "Here's what I want to do. I'm going to ad-lib the entire thing."

Amazingly, he said, "Sure, whatever you want."

He could've said, "I don't know what you think you're doing, but you're not bringing me down with you. If you want to make a fool out of yourself, good luck with that."

But I knew it would work.

Starting with my very first sports segment in Hartford in 1974, when I ad-libbed my entire segment, that was what I did every night, and it continued when I went to Philadelphia and then on to San Diego.

According to the ratings and market research, which is all that matters in this business, my sports segments were getting attention.

On weekends, I'd go to Cape Cod, a popular vacation getaway for Hartford, and wherever I went, you would've thought I was anchoring at a Boston station.

I'd walk down the street and it was, "You're Ted Leitner, right? We love watching you!"

I couldn't walk 10 feet without signing an autograph, which I didn't mind. I was stunned.

I'd never had such recognition in my life, certainly not in Oklahoma City. I couldn't help but think, "Wow, this is unbelievable, it must be working."

Before I arrived, Hartford's TV sportscasters were a bunch of old radio guys or retired jocks doing sports on TV, looking up and down in a monotone delivery, with absolutely no personality.

And here was this idiot, me, just talking conversationally to viewers, ad-libbing everything, and tossing out my attempts at irreverent humor. Not everything worked, but enough did.

The station's execs kept getting letters and phone calls about me that usually said things like, "Listen, I don't know much about sports, but I love that new guy who's now doing your sports."

There was even a perfume-scented letter from a young woman who wrote, "I love his smile" and "I love his hands, he has such beautiful hands" – all this crazy stuff that my bosses absolutely loved.

After a while, they said, "OK, we get it. Keep doing what you're doing. Do whatever you want to do."

And that's what I did.

Back when I had dark hair and big glasses in Oklahoma City. Think the lapels are wide enough on that stylish sport coat?

22

A big, big mistake

"These women aren't here for me, are they?"

W<small>HEN</small> I <small>GOT TO</small> WFSB-TV <small>IN</small> H<small>ARTFORD</small>, I had a three-year contract, but only the first year was guaranteed.

Then, there was supposed to be a six-month extension that would have to be picked up after that first year.

What happened was, I discovered that the news director somehow forgot to extend my contract, thus violating the terms of our original deal. All of a sudden, I was no longer bound by that contract.

I didn't have an agent – never have – but I thought I owed it to myself to make a few calls to see what else might be out there.

After word got out that I was available, I got a call from WCBS-TV in New York. The news director, Eric Ober, who later was my boss in Philadelphia and after that became president of CBS News, said he knew my work and was interested in meeting with me.

Same thing with KRON-TV in San Francisco, where the news director said he'd heard about me and asked for a tape.

Then I got a call from a corporate headhunter who said WCAU-TV in Philadelphia was looking for a sports guy who didn't do the standard "scores and highlights" like everyone else.

So, I had three big-time stations in big-market cities – New York City, San Francisco, and Philadelphia – in a bidding war for my services.

After weighing my options, which were generous for that time, I agreed to go to Philadelphia, which turned out to be a big, big mistake.

As mentioned, my new boss, Eric Ober, assured me that he really did want someone "offbeat."

But I've got news for you – sports fans in Philadelphia don't like offbeat. They take their sports seriously, way too seriously.

You don't joke about the Flyers, and you don't joke about the "Igles" or the "Phiwies," as the locals called them.

Like an idiot, I went to Philly with my shtick and after a month or so, a voice in the back of my head started saying, louder and louder, "This ain't working. They don't *like* you."

I never felt very comfortable in Philadelphia and I shouldn't have taken the job. These were the same "fans" who booed and heckled Santa Claus at an Eagles game back in 1968, and pelted him with snowballs.

They were same "fans" who, in the words of the late comic David Brenner, would go to the airport and boo bad landings.

Throughout my time there, about 18 months, I'd be thinking, "What am I doing here?"

But the money was nice and I got to work the Eagles' exhibition games with guys like Tom Brookshier and Irv Cross and the legendary Chuck Bednarik, even Paul Hornung.

Sometimes, that was enough.

I'll never forget doing an Eagles-Packers preseason game from Green Bay's Lambeau Field with Paul Hornung, not so much for the game itself, but for the spectacle that "The Golden Boy" caused wherever he went.

After our pre-game production meeting, about 90 minutes before game-time, Paul said to me, "Why don't we take a walk?"

We started walking through the main concourse and you would've thought I was with Mick Jagger *and* Michael Jackson.

It was "Paul! Paul! Paul!"

I'd never seen anything like that in my life. It was incredible.

He was having a great time, shaking hands and signing autographs and giving all the pretty girls hugs and more hugs. I looked at him and said, "Oh, so *that's* what it's like to be a star."

We laughed and laughed, because that's what your life was like when you were the great Paul Hornung, a legendary ladies' man who also happened to be one of the greatest running backs in NFL history.

After the game, there were, let's say, *lots* of younger women standing outside the press box, waiting for the game to end.

As Paul and I walked out, I turned to him and said: "Hey, Paul, these women aren't here for me, are they?"

"Nope."

Back in Philadelphia, Tom Brookshier, the Eagles' former All-Pro who was very popular in Philly for a long time, was also doing CBS' Game of the Week with Pat Summerall, pairing two NFL greats in the booth.

Just before the season started, "Brooky" took an offer to go full-time with the network as an analyst.

His departure gave me the 6 o'clock *and* the 11 o'clock sports segments, in the nation's fifth-largest media market. Pretty good opportunity, right?

But, unlike when I was in Hartford, it was obvious that Philadelphia's sports fans didn't care for me – not at all. Can you imagine that?

The station's research on viewers' reaction to my sports segment was less than enthusiastic. Way less. The station got complaints that I was too sarcastic, too opinionated, and that I didn't worship Philly's teams like I was supposed to.

Not only that, my boss kept saying, "Stop smiling, our research says it bothers our viewers. They're saying, 'What are you smiling about?' What's so funny, anyway?"

To summarize: Smiling in Hartford? OK.

Smiling in Philadelphia? *Not* OK.

I told him, "You've got the wrong guy."

Whatever I did in Oklahoma City and Hartford had worked, but it was an utter disaster in Philadelphia.

Thank God, it worked in San Diego.

23

All those lunatics

"Hey, what am I supposed to do here?"

When I was in Philadelphia, my worst on-air experience, among many, went way beyond crazy.

It was in 1977, when the Phillies were playing the Dodgers in the National League playoffs. The WCAU-TV technical crew had set up a remote truck outside Veterans Stadium for a live shot after Game 3.

The series was tied at one game apiece, with a classic pitching matchup, the Phillies' Steve Carlton going against the Dodgers' Burt Hooten, the target of the Phillies fans' obnoxious razzing.

The Phillies carried a 5-3 lead into the top of the 9th, but blew it when the visiting Dodgers scored three runs, beating the Phillies, 6-5.

The next day at Veterans Stadium, the Dodgers clinched the pennant.

But for me, the real action took place after the Phillies' loss in Game 3, when I was scheduled to lead the 11 o'clock news with our post-game report.

It was clear to us that these "fans" were absolutely hell-bent on doing serious property damage and personal damage as they roamed the parking lot – bending off car antennas, scratching cars with their keys, starting fights, you know, the usual Philadelphia "fan" insanity.

We could tell they were gathering by the dozens, then hundreds, then a few thousand, all of them pissed off, drawn to our remote truck like the vermin they were.

About 15 minutes before our 11 o'clock air-time, one of our remote crew guys who knew I wasn't a favorite of WCAU viewers, looked at me and said, "Uh-oh, man. If you keep standing here, it'll be a mob scene and you'll get knocked over. You'd better climb up top – now."

Not being a total idiot, at least that time, I climbed up the truck's side ladder, despite my fear of heights.

That led to an open area on top of the truck, where the portable satellite dish was, creating a "studio" that provided at least some protection. Looking out at that mob was a scary sight.

I also remember that game because, early on, the "fans" had riled up Hooton with a rising crescendo of catcalls and screaming.

It got to the point where he held his hands up, palms outstretched, as if to say, "For Christ's sake, I can't hear myself think!" as he walked back to the mound after one of his pitches.

Hooten then objected to a handful of home plate ump Harry Wendelstedt's close calls. That inflamed the "fans" even more, with chants of "Hoot, Hoot, Hoot" causing Hooten to lose it.

Of course, the crazies got even louder and more obnoxious.

Now, these same crazies have surrounded us and they're rocking the truck back and forth, and I'm on top of the truck, trying to keep my balance by holding onto the side railing.

I held on tight with one hand while I continued to do the

sports and narrated the highlights while watching the monitor, with the truck swaying back and forth.

Not fun. Not funny.

I remember thinking, "Please, God, let me end this segment without a fractured skull when I fall off the top of this truck."

Thankfully, I didn't experience anything like that again until the Padres went to Detroit for the final two games of the 1984 World Series.

That time, I was situated with our Channel 8 news crew on top of an old church, looking down at the front of Tiger Stadium with all these lunatics rioting and burning cars, even police cars, and throwing bottles at mounted police officers.

That was a true riot and their team had just won the 1984 World Series.

Lucky for me, they had no chance to get to me or anybody else in our crew. Not so lucky were the group of Padres fans stuck in a tour bus that rioters came close to turning over.

It didn't take long before I fully realized I had picked the wrong market by going to Philadelphia. I knew it wasn't working, and so did management.

After a year and a half, the station's general manager and news director invited me to join them for lunch. That's usually not a good sign.

Before we ordered, the GM asked me, "Tell me, Ted, do you dive?"

"What do you mean 'dive'"?

"You know, in the ocean. Scuba, that sort of thing."

"No, never done it, never had any interest in doing it."

"Well, let me put it this way: After our last marketing research, you give our audience the bends."

So, I said, "Well, guys, it appears I'm on the menu today. Why don't we just order lunch and I'll start sending out my tapes and calling around. How's that?"

After they nodded their approval, I added, "Listen, you don't have to fire me. I understand what's going on. I was the wrong guy. Your headhunter was wrong. You *didn't* want off-beat, so you didn't want me."

"Believe me," I added, "I get it."

Ever heard of that cable comedy show, *It's Always Sunny in Philadelphia*?

It wasn't all that sunny for me.

It was time to move on.

24

Junior Seau, Part 1

"It's obvious that you have no idea what you're talking about."

I FIRST GOT TO KNOW TIAINA BAUL SEAU – Junior Seau – after I'd been at Channel 8 in San Diego a few years, around May of 1990.

Surprisingly, he called me asking for advice on how he should handle what was turning out to be a nasty contract negotiation with the Chargers.

Possibly at the direction of team owner Alex Spanos, then-general manager Bobby Beathard was being a hard-ass in their initial contract talks after the Chargers selected him from USC as their No. 1 choice and fifth overall in the NFL Draft.

Of course, Junior had been an all-CIF player at Oceanside High and then USC, even after missing his freshman year because his entrance exams made him ineligible to play that first season.

A few weeks after he'd been drafted by the Chargers, Junior started calling me after I'd wrapped up my 6 pm segment and sometimes later, after my 11 pm segment. By that time, I was pretty tired and looking forward to going home.

But talking to Junior was always a kick.

He'd say: "Ted, I need your advice on how I should handle this, not so much from the money standpoint, but the PR standpoint. I don't get it."

I told him: "Junior, I know what you're talking about. Fans always take the side of management rather than the player in these things."

"Yeah, why is that?"

I said, "I don't know, Junior. It's like they played some high school football, so they've played the game – not at your level, not at all – but they think you're just like they are and you shouldn't make that kind of money, because they don't."

That's always bugged me about sports fans. Somehow, they're jealous that top athletes get paid millions to play the sport that fans once played, and as a result, they always side with the billionaire owners.

It's always been that way, but it doesn't make any sense.

And if you were a Channel 8 viewer, you're probably thinking, hey, Big Mouth, you did the same thing ranting and raving about all the high salaries those guys were making back then.

You're right, I did.

But I didn't begrudge them because I'd rather they make "big coin" than wealthy team owners.

When Junior and Gina were featured in the Sports Illustrated swimsuit issue years later, it was around the time of a banquet that I MC'ed for the Seau Foundation.

In the dining room, they had posted some of those incredible poses of NFL players, including Junior, and their wives, so I told the banquet, "After all these years of seeing Junior and that incredible body, who would've thought that all this time Junior had only the second-best body in his own house."

Here's what I told Junior: "Listen, from a PR standpoint, you're going to take your lumps. Some fans are going to think you're selfish because you want to be paid what you think you're worth."

"Maybe some of your own teammates will think the same thing."

Finally, I told him: "But, Junior, you've got to do what you've got to do for yourself and your family."

I was certain he would take care of his extended family and his friends because that's what a Samoan kid does who has the character like he had.

As things turned out, he did financially support a lot of people, probably too many. But he was very concerned that he might go from hometown hero to selfish ingrate and risk getting booed by fans who thought he made too much money.

That didn't happen because of his generous nature and the kind of all-out, absolutely terrific player he was.

The other conversations Junior and I had aired every Friday and Monday throughout the NFL season. We paid him to do a Q&A segment with me on Channel 8.

He was the Samoan Don Rickles, insulting me and putting me down with that sly smile of his. Our viewers loved it.

"Well, Ted," he'd say, "it's obvious that you have no idea what you're talking about. Really, what *do* you know, anyway?"

Our risk-taking news director, Jim Holtzman, who had

hired me along with Michael Tuck and Allison Ross back in the late 1970s, loved it.

"Keep doing that, it's great stuff, our viewers love it," he'd say.

And I'd say, "Hey, I'm not doing it, Junior's doing it."

I remember when Junior's then-wife Gina, who had previously worked for the Chargers, would come with him to the station, holding their newborn daughter, Sydney.

Later, in 2011, when he was posthumously inducted into the Pro Football Hall of Fame, that baby girl was now 21 and all grown up, poised and beautiful and eloquent.

I thought to myself, "I held that baby and now there she is, introducing my friend, Junior, who left us way too soon."

WE'LL BE RIGHT BACK AFTER THESE WORDS

PART 6

"You couldn't even squeeze a wing in there!"

Back when I was single and living in Philadelphia, that's when the NFL had local TV blackouts, even for preseason games.

That meant our Eagles' telecasts were delayed until after the game, usually at 11 pm.

Lucky for me, I had arranged an after-game dinner date and she later invited me to come over to her place.

As we were getting to know each other better, she happened to turn on the TV, which was tuned to the Eagles delayed telecast. There I was, scoring with my new honey – while also critiquing my play-by-play call.

Now, I can't help thinking about that D.Z. Akin's TV commercial, the one where I'm sitting in a booth, waiting for my meal to be brought to me.

When the waiter finally sets down my favorite order, I throw my arms in the arms like I'd just scored a touchdown and then shout, "SCORRRE!"

One summer while I was going to Oklahoma State and working summers in Wellington, Kansas, that was the first time I'd been on my own for any extended period of time.

I was impressed when I saw a TV ad for a new product

called Shake 'N Bake, which came in a cardboard box with everything you'd ever need to make your home-cooked chicken taste great.

The ad showed the chicken frying in the pan, delicious and nothing but easy to prepare.

The mom says, "We used Shake 'N Bake."

And her little girl next to her says, "And I helped."

Well, she didn't help *me* much.

I brought a box of Shake 'N Bake, took it home, opened the pouch and, I swear to you, I started to look for the chicken – a thigh or a breast, *something* – that I just knew had to come in that box.

But no chicken.

It never occurred to me to think, "Look at the box. See how small it is? You couldn't even squeeze a wing in there!"

I've never been much of a homemaker.

The late Tug McGraw, who came up with the phrase, "Ya gotta believe" with the "Miracle Mets" of 1973, was never at a loss for words.

By the time I got to Philadelphia, the left-handed reliever known for his quick wit and offbeat antics, was with the Phillies.

Asked what he would do with his signing bonus, Tug, who lived for a time in Poway, said, "I'm gonna spend 90% of it on women and Irish whisky and probably just waste the rest."

Asked why he had bought a used 1960s car, Tug replied, "Because it plays great oldies."

Clearly, music appreciation runs in the family. Tug's son, country star Tim McGraw, is famously married to another country star, the lovely Faith Hill.

Like I said, I've never considered myself real bright.

You want some examples?

When I was walking on the beach with a female friend in Puerto Vallarta, we were talking about altitudes in the nearby mountains. I asked her, "What's the altitude *here*?"

Another time, I was with a female friend who was a professional photographer, way back when they had darkrooms before the digital age.

She was complaining to me about how sick and tired she was, being stuck in that darkroom, where it has to be kept completely dark or else the film would be ruined.

She said, "I listen to the radio, but I get sick of that."

And I said, "Why don't you put a TV in there?"

I told that story at a meeting of radio sales people, most of whom were young, and there was nothing but crickets.

I said, "Wait a minute, you're too young. You don't even know what a darkroom is!"

Keeping score with broadcast partner Dave "Soupy" Campbell, who knew his baseball and later went to ESPN and the Colorado Rockies.

25

Some wild-eyed lunatic

"They're gonna hate me before they even see me."

WHEN I FIRST GOT TO SAN DIEGO, it was early January 1978 and Channel 8 put me up in the Hyatt Islandia overlooking Mission Bay.

I'd been here a few years before, while doing an exhibition game with the Philadelphia Eagles as the play-by-play guy.

I checked into my room, and right away, I turned on Channel 8, figuring I'd see what I'd gotten myself into.

After a few minutes or so, I saw this promo touting "the new guy," except it didn't show me at all.

Instead, it was some guy who was rifling through this big box filled with different balls – baseballs, footballs, basketballs, with golf clubs, hockey sticks, tennis rackets, and ice skates.

The promo copy and narration was about how outrageous "the new guy" is, how different and funny he is.

I thought, "Oh, please don't do that to me."

It'd be like introducing a new standup comic no one's ever

heard of, with the MC saying, "Believe me, this guy is really, really funny. Now, here he is ... OK, you jerk, be funny!"

Not good.

To heighten the suspense, I guess, the promo didn't show any video of me, nothing, didn't even mention my name. Only that, "He's coming," starting January 30, if I recall.

I thought, "That's strike one against you. They're gonna expect some wild-eyed lunatic who bounces off the walls."

Then I thought, "They're going to hate me before they even see me," which, thank God, wasn't totally the case.

That reminded me of another *M*A*S*H* line when Frank, in lamenting to Trapper, said, "Why does everyone take such an instant dislike to me?"

Trapper says, "It saves time, Frank."

That could've been me.

For the longest time, whenever I'd do banquets and presentations – and I did thousands of them – KFMB's Hudson & Bauer morning show listeners would greet me by saying in a shrill voice, "HOUSSSSSE KEEPING!!"

That was the catch-phrase of one of our most popular routines, where I'd come back from a road trip and Mac or Joe would ask me, "So, how'd your trip go?"

I'd go on a rant about how, in every hotel I've ever stayed in, I've always put out that little door-hanger sign, the one that says, DO NOT DISTURB, for all to see.

Yet, every morning, I'd get a knock at the door while I was still sound asleep, because I'm far from an early riser. Not even close.

I'd hear a loud knock and then, "HOUSSSSSSE KEEPING!!"

The door would open and I'd be face-to-face with a hotel

maid who was intent on cleaning my room and making my bed – with me in it.

I'd try to be nice about it, so I'd say, "Ma'am, the sign's right there. What part of Do Not Disturb do you not understand?"

I realize these people work their butts off, and I'd never abuse them in any way. But the reason I put the sign on the doorknob was so I wouldn't be disturbed – like the sign said.

Then she'd ask, "Would you like me to clean your room?"

"No, I'm good."

"Do you have enough towels?"

"Lady, I got enough towels in here to last me for *two weeks*."

Wherever I go on the road, I hear the same thing – "HOUSSSSSSE KEEPING!!" – and it still DRIVES ME CRAZY!

During a Clippers' road trip, I was talking to guard Randy Smith about how housekeepers would always just knock and a few seconds later, open the door with their key.

Randy came up with temporary fix for that situation.

After the knock, he dropped trou, jumped on top of the bed, crossed his arms and said, "Come in."

She came in, poor girl, and screamed! Then she ran away.

Randy said he never had a problem again, at least not at that hotel.

In my first year at Channel 8, KFMB Radio's general manager Paul Palmer came to me before the football season and asked, "Hey, have you ever done any college football and basketball play-by-play?"

"Yeah, why?"

"Well, I'm hiring Eddie Doucette to replace Ron Reina to

do San Diego State football and basketball" – this was after they had fired Ron, which really hurt me because everyone who knew Ron liked him.

Paul told me he was getting ready to hire Doucette, a nationally known NBA guy with good credentials who was leaving the Milwaukee Bucks' play-by-play job.

But at the last moment, Eddie decided to wait another year, so Paul came to me, asking if I'd like to do Aztecs play-by-play, which I regarded as a great opportunity.

I said, "I'll do it," and that became another break for my career. It was like one thing happened after the next – like that 1950s movie based on the life of boxer Rocky Graziano, *Somebody Up There Likes Me*.

That's been me, my entire career.

———— ∝∞∝ ————

On Hudson & Bauer – hosted by two terrific pros, Mac Hudson and Joe Bauer – my segments were supposed to be a five-minute morning sports update at 7:15 and again at 8:15.

For those segments, we'd blow past the scheduled five-minute mark because I'd just keep talking. We were having too much fun.

Right away, our comic instincts just meshed and we became a big hit with listeners – even more importantly, with our bill-paying sponsors.

For the first H&B show I did, just before they introduced me, Mac was laughing like a maniac about something that had happened minutes before.

Mac had this great laugh, an uncontrollable laugh like when you were kids in school or in church, when you knew you couldn't keep from laughing, even when you knew you would get in trouble.

Believe me, I know that feeling.

So, he was still laughing and then he introduced me: "Now, here's a brand-new segment. Here's Ted Leitner from Channel 8 with Sports and he's going to be doing a segment with us, starting today, every morning at 7:15 and 8:15."

I came on, and said, "Hey, Mac, wanna do me a favor?"

"Sure, what's that?"

"Cheer up."

He started laughing again, hysterically. We didn't stop laughing for the next 20 years, until Mac, who was prone to alcohol abuse, died way too soon, at 58.

Such a loss.

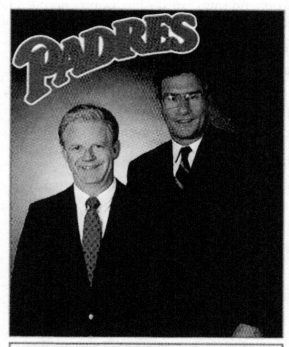

Padres Announcers 76
Bob Chandler-Ted Leitner

A promotional ad from the early years, when Bob Chandler and I handled the Padres' Cox telecasts. The guy on the left really knows his baseball.

26

An amazing proposal

*"We ate together, we drank together,
we partied together."*

Aɴʏ ᴛɪᴍᴇ ʏᴏᴜ'ʀᴇ ᴅɪғғᴇʀᴇɴᴛ ɪɴ TV, it's a case of viewers thinking to themselves as they watch you, "Do I hate him?" or, "Do I love him?"

As long as I was at Channel 8, I'm grateful that it was more love than hate.

Mostly.

A year or so into my contract, I had a meeting with Bob Myers, then-CEO of KFMB's TV and radio stations.

He started out by saying, "Ted, our marketing research shows that 60% of our news audience says you're the reason they watch our newscasts."

Right away, I said with a laugh, "Bob, you shouldn't have told me that. You know my contract's coming up for renewal pretty soon, right?"

Bob said, "Hey, I don't care. I'm going to pay you what you should get and as long as you don't go to Channel 39 or Channel 10 or Channel 6, I'll pay you what you're worth to us."

Besides mentioning those local stations, what he was really referring to, and I knew it, was the generous offer I had just turned down from WABC/Channel 7 in New York, which I seriously considered.

I mean, why wouldn't I?

After Warner Wolf, one of the most innovative TV sports guys in our business, left WABC and moved to WCBS/Channel 2 for a reported $1 million a year, the WABC execs must've said after seeing my tapes, "Hey, he's a lot like Warner. Let's go after him."

At their invitation, I happily flew from San Diego to Hilton Head Island, off the coast of South Carolina, where they had booked an executive R&R getaway, to conveniently get out of the New York City winter.

We met at this ritzy resort and they offered me a lot of money to do sports on WABC's early and late newscasts. As added incentive, they tossed in a first-class, round-trip ticket every month so that I'd be able to see my son, who was living in Orange County at the time.

It was an amazing proposal.

So, I went to Bob Myers and told him about the offer.

A few days later, I heard from someone in KFMB's sales department that word had leaked out that I might be headed to New York. To them, it was a case of, "We've got clients saying they won't renew with us until they find out whether you're staying or going."

That didn't hurt me at all, so Bob Myers came back to me with a revised and much more generous offer. Needless to say, the numbers made it easier to stay, as I was also doing the Padres' and the Aztecs' play-by-play by that time, early in 1981.

Channel 8 was able to make its offer based on the revenue from some truly unbelievable Nielsen ratings, the kind of numbers that hardly ever happen, anywhere, no matter the market.

Believe me, it was by no means only me. We had just the right combination of on-air talent and management – both in radio and TV – that made us unbeatable.

C'mon, I was with an on-air team led by Michael Tuck, Allison Ross, Clark Anthony, plus Larry Himmel, and later, Hal Clement and Marty Levin, and a terrific stable of reporters. On the radio side, it was Hudson & Bauer mornings, Mark Larson afternoons, and Bill Ballance at night. This was big-time talent.

What fun we had.

We ate together, we drank together, and we partied together. It was incredible, with executives like Bob Myers, Paul Palmer, Mark Larson, and Jim Holtzman. It was, indeed, a family that worked together and played together.

I look back at those years and think, "My God, that was so wonderful."

The truth is that Jim Holtzman was the "father" of News Eight and, quite frankly, directly responsible for my success.

After he came to Channel 8 in 1977, he hired all of us – me, Michael Tuck, Allison Ross, Clark Anthony, Larry Himmel, Hal Clement, Loren Nancarrow, et al.

He also inherited a 90-minute nightly newscast that was ratings loser, far behind the competition.

Soon enough, he turned News Eight into the market's top station, generating ratings that were unheard of, not only at that time but since.

Along the way, he added a 6:30 pm newscast and gave his full support to *San Diego At Large* – a nightly 30-minute sketch comedy series hosted by Larry Himmel (remember "The Adventures of Biff & Skippy"?) that was unlike anything local TV had ever seen.

For me, he was a godsend.

Jim not only got me to come to San Diego, but he truly "got" me and what I was doing on air. What's more, he encouraged it.

He knew people were watching and either agreeing, disagreeing, liking or hating me. But they were watching, and he wanted me to stir up the audience for that very reason.

Many times when I passed his office on the way to the studio, he would yell to me, "Get out there and piss 'em off!"

If you think you're a big talent, you ain't nothin' without your boss having your back.

Jim had mine, always.

Contrast that with my friend Chris Berman's experience in ESPN's early years. He'd be doing his crazy nicknames and his boss would tell him, "Not funny. Knock it off."

Of course, he didn't.

Instead, nicknames like Bert "Be Home" Blyleven, Oddibe "Young Again" McDowell, Rollie "Chicken" Fingers and so many others made him different and he became ESPN's biggest star for years.

Same with the late Stuart Scott.

One executive genius told him, "Most of our audience isn't Black and they don't talk like you with your 'boo-yah' and other expressions. Stop it."

Just like Boomer, he stood up to that nonsense. He did it his way and made it big.

There was none of that executive selective involvement for me at Channel 8. I had Jim's total support.

Thank you, Jim Holtzman, for my professional life.

———— ✺ ————

What I'm proud of, despite that love-hate situation when I was on Channel 8 and KFMB, was that people got the impression that I was telling the truth.

When I would go out on a limb with a commentary, such as when I said that James Harris wasn't playing as much as he should because he was a Black quarterback.

That was back in the time when many people in coaching didn't think Blacks were smart enough to be a quarterback or a center.

By doing those kinds of commentaries, I think it established that, no matter who it was or who it ticked off, I was going to be honest – even if it hurt my career.

When I started doing radio commercials, around the time I was doing my radio shows in the 1990s, it benefited me that my listeners would buy the products that I was advertising.

Because they thought I was honest.

The greeter at Marvin K. Brown Cadillac told me one time about a guy who came into the dealership and bought an Eldorado for about $50,000.

He told the salesman, "I heard Leitner's commercial and I don't even like him. But he tells the truth and I trust him. He said, come to Marvin K. Brown – and here I am."

That sort of thing really helped me. And it does to this day, in my association with SONIC drive-ins and Kearny Mesa Subaru and Hyundai.

———— ✺ ————

I couldn't possibly say enough wonderful things about Joan Kroc, who took over the Padres' ownership after her husband,

McDonald's founder, Ray, died on January 4, 1984, the year that turned out to be the Padres' first-ever World Series.

Joan was a very, very special person.

One night, by invitation, I went to her home for a dinner party, about a dozen invited guests. Of course, her home in Rancho Santa Fe was a showcase.

As we sat down at this huge dinner table, I noticed off the side that there was a riser with a drum set, a bass and piano.

But because the invitation hadn't mentioned anything about musical entertainment of any sort, I figured Joan must be setting up for another party.

After dinner, we all moved to her spacious living room. Then Joan stood up on that riser, welcomed us with her usual charm, then said with a flourish, "Now, my friends, here's Tony Bennett."

The great Tony Bennett came striding down the hall in a tuxedo and he played and sang brilliantly for the next two hours.

Then he chatted with us for an hour in the living room.

And I thought to myself, more than few times, what's this schmuck from New York doing here? Imagine, I grew up with next to nothing, and because I talked about sports for a living, at this moment I was listening in-person to Tony Bennett, one of my all-time favorite artists.

What did I do to deserve this?

Here's a story I've told at corporate events and college business classes.

In any negotiation, you've got to know who the "power person" is.

As in, who's going to make the final decision? And what's the hot button to push to get the deal?

Back in the 1980s, KFMB Radio had the Padres' radio rights, and XTRA Sports 690 wanted them. Badly. So much so that they outbid us by over a million dollars.

They concentrated on negotiating with Padres club president Dick Freeman, while KFMB's Paul Palmer knew he had an "in."

At the final presentation, 690 came in with a giant blowup of a check for a million bucks, while Palmer carried a giant teddy bear.

His pitch was simple, "We don't have that kind of money, but I'll tell you what we *do* have. We have a family ... the KFMB and Padres family ... warm and cozy, just like this bear and it's not all about the money.

"We've got Hudson & Bauer and we've got Ted Leitner. We've been family and together for years and we've always had this warm, cozy feeling."

Sitting there was Joan Beverly Kroc – Padres owner, philanthropist, billionaire – who listened to H&B every morning. Often, she'd quote back to me the things I'd said on that morning's segments.

Not that she liked everything I said back then, such as, "The Padres are in collusion with the other owners to not sign free agents."

After she heard that, she called club president Ballard Smith and shouted, "Do *we* pay Ted?"

"Yes."

"*WHY?!*"

After the presentation, Joan called me later at my home, and said, "A million dollars? I've spent that on jewelry in a week! They thought I would care about money? It was *OVER!*"

And that's how KFMB retained the rights to broadcast Padres baseball.

Palmer knew what buttons to push and what motivated the true decision-maker.

A classic lesson of Business 101.

27

Junior Seau, Part 2

"Believe me, I tried and tried and tried."

A FEW WEEKS AFTER JUNIOR SEAU tried to commit suicide by driving his SUV off a Carlsbad beachfront cliff in the early morning hours of October 18, 2010, we got together for dinner at his Mission Valley offices.

The setting was the second story of his restaurant called, appropriately enough, SEAU's The Restaurant.

Looking back, I'm sorry to say that neither of us were self-reflective enough to put two-and-two together, that is, to fully realize what was going on in his life.

When I asked him about the "accident," he told me the same thing he told everyone else, including the police, that he had simply fallen asleep at the wheel. He was, as it turned out, distraught after being arrested on a domestic violence charge, filed by his then-wife Gina.

His life by that point was clearly a mess, filled with alcohol and painkiller abuse, bouts of uncontrolled rage, depression, and bizarre behavior. But few of us outside his close-knit orbit were able to see it that way.

Of course, I didn't know what some of his family members and friends knew about his deteriorating state, that, as one example, when he'd see his kids, he'd just sit there and stare at the TV without paying any attention to them.

But the TV wasn't on.

Those were the behaviors that were unknown to those of us outside his circle. We just didn't have any idea what he was going through.

Those revelations, and many more, came out later in *Junior Seau: The Life and Death of a Football Icon*, an excellent book by ESPN's Jim Trotter, formerly of the *San Diego Union-Tribune*, published three years after Junior's death.

In his book, Trotter wrote that Junior would come to his restaurant and tell the manager in a blind rage, "Hey, what are all these people doing in my restaurant? Get them out of here!"

That alone should've been a red-flag warning of what was going on and, worse, what was to come.

My only excuse is that I had absolutely no idea those things were going on. So, I never regarded his first suicide attempt as anything but an unfortunate accident.

I was wrong.

So, Junior and I are enjoying this delicious dinner that his staff brought up from the kitchen for us and we're having a wonderful time, laughing and joking with each other, just like we used to do in the Channel 8 days when we'd do our TV segments and he'd rip me a new one.

At one point, I teased him, saying, "Hey, June, nice driving, very nice. My son is going to start driving soon. Maybe you could give him lessons?"

I'm laughing and he's laughing and I have no reason to think that what I'm hearing him say is not even close to his true reality – which was an attempted suicide. I'm sure of that now.

Later, as we shared war stories about the old days, I pointed to the cracked Chargers helmet that Junior very conspicuously displayed on his desk.

The three-inch crack was the result of a collision with Chargers running back Fred McCrary, who was the lead blocker in a preseason training camp scrimmage in 2001.

Going full-force as usual, Junior met McCrary helmet-to-helmet and I'm sure that resulted in one of the 1,500 or so concussions that Gary Plummer, Junior's former Chargers teammate, believes Junior suffered in his playing career.

According to Trotter's account, both Junior and McCrary cracked their helmets in that collision. And both proudly displayed them after their careers were over.

When I mentioned that helmet, Junior was only too happy to give me the backstory, how it happened, how proud he was of that moment, and so on.

Looking back, I just loved every second of that night at SEAU's, catching up with the Junior we all thought we knew.

That was the last time I saw him alive.

—— ⌘ ——

Some two years after Junior committed suicide by shooting himself in the heart – sparing his brain, which was traumatized by the damaging effects of Chronic Traumatic Encephalopathy (CTE) – I was talking in the Qualcomm Stadium press box with Aaron Taylor, the former Packers and Chargers tackle.

We were both doing an Aztecs game, me for the Aztecs, Aaron for CBS Sports.

We got to talking about Junior and Trotter's sad, revelatory book and I asked Aaron, who was a close friend of Junior's, "Did you have any idea?"

"I had an idea only about the alcohol," he said. "I'm a recovering alcoholic and I was always trying to get Junior to get into a program. But he would always blow me off. I knew that if you kept bugging him about anything, you were no longer his friend. With Junior, it was always that way.

"Believe me, I tried."

Taylor went on: "I knew his attitude was part of what he was going through, post-football, but I wasn't yet fully aware about the extent of CTE."

And I said, "Well, who of us was?"

I think back to my dinner with Junior, how I teased him about the accident when, clearly, he tried to kill himself, and my heart breaks.

Distressed, I said to Aaron, "Man, how could I have said that?"

And he told me, "Don't get down on yourself. We all said things that we now regret. We just didn't know."

Then I remember seeing that dramatic footage of Junior's mom, the woman he lovingly called "homegirl," as his body was being taken away in a medical examiner's van, only hours after the suicide.

Terribly distraught, she was almost running after the van as it drove away, and she cried out several times, "Junior, why didn't you tell me? I would have gone with you."

That broke my heart.

Junior Seau was a proud Samoan warrior of the highest, toughest order and I respected him so much.

28

Go wake him up

"I never knew what they were going to ask."

W<small>HAT MOST SURPRISED ME</small> about doing those early-morning segments on Hudson & Bauer was that they were early in the morning, *much* too early.

I've always been a bad morning guy.

In my fraternity at Oklahoma State, we'd have, let's say, 50 guys and 25 rooms and you couldn't set a wake-up alarm for each one of us because alarms would be going off all the time, waking up guys who didn't have to wake up.

So, they'd have the pledges wake up the brothers at whatever time you requested by putting your name on a sign-up list.

My frat brother would look at the list and say, "Is Leitner on there?"

"Yeah."

"Go wake him up."

They were pulling a prank on the pledge because what they didn't say was, "He'll tear your head off. Don't do it! He puts his name on the list and then he says, '*Get out of here!*' and goes back to sleep and cuts class."

That's how bad I was at waking up early, or anything close to early.

I was being offered what I thought was a wonderful morning show with a couple of funny, talented guys, and it was easy for me to say, "Of course, count me in."

Money was not that big of a factor for those early-morning segments, and neither was doing Aztecs football and basketball. But I loved doing both gigs, and still love broadcasting the Aztecs.

With what I was making from Channel 8 and my radio talk shows, I was doing just fine and didn't need to strong-arm the Aztecs. Besides, I knew that San Diego State's athletic department didn't have a lot of money, and I didn't want to squeeze them for more.

I still make pretty much the same per-game stipend now that I made in the early 1980s, doing Aztecs football and basketball, because I've always done it as my contribution to the program all these years.

❦

On Channel 8, we used to have a segment called "Hey, Ted," in which a random viewer would ask me a question and I'd do my best to answer it on the air.

It was good TV, plus it made my adrenaline flow because I never knew what they were going to ask.

Early on, one of the questions – actually, an accusation – went something like, "Ted, you do show hockey highlights, but you don't really show the game highlights. You only show the fights."

Then someone else would say: "You do the same thing with auto racing. You say, 'Here are the highlights,' and you'll show like two seconds of the traffic on I-5."

I'd say, "OK, here's tonight's hockey highlights," and I'd show those classic NHL fights where everyone drops their sticks and gloves and they go at it.

I've always thought hockey fights were nothing but idiotic. Rodney Dangerfield was right when he said he went to a boxing match and a hockey game broke out.

Then I'd come back and say, "I must apologize, because I really didn't do a good narration.

"I should've told you that, for ID purposes, Moron No. 1 was on the left and that was Moron No. 2 on the right. I just needed to make that clear."

I was making good money, and I was working with people I loved, and my shtick was working. We were getting big ratings – I mean, *big* ratings.

Another reason we had such good ratings, besides the actual newscasts, was that we had two straight classic episodes of *M*A*S*H*, one of my all-time favorite shows, airing at 4 and again at 4:30, as our lead-ins.

During that time period, we had a 14 rating, which meant that 14 percent of all homes in San Diego at that time were tuned to Channel 8, which was unheard of then and certainty not now.

It also meant the station was generating some serious ad dollars.

In the 1990s, I happened to meet the creator of *M*A*S*H*, the brilliant Larry Gelbart, at a Dodgers-Padres game at Dodger Stadium.

The introduction came from Ken Levine, a very talented director, producer and writer – with *M*A*S*H, Cheers, Frasier* and *The Simpsons* among his many credits – who also did Padres' radio play-by-play for a few years in the mid-1990s.

After Ken introduced me to Larry, I grabbed Larry's hand and kissed his ring.

Was Gelbart funny?

He was writing comedy for network radio shows in New York when he was 16 and still in high school.

I said, "Larry, let me tell you something I'd like you to know. Not only do I love *M*A*S*H*, and not only are you a brilliant creator and writer, but thank you, thank you for my TV news career."

WE'LL BE RIGHT BACK AFTER THESE WORDS

PART 7

"But what about the interest?"

And now, herrrrrre's Rickey....

Rickey Henderson was getting on the Padres' team bus, which by tradition had the most senior player in the first row, on the left side, as you get on the bus.

Rickey was about to sit down in that seat, but Steve Finley was already sitting there.

Rickey looked at Finley and said, "Hey, what're you doing in my seat?"

Finley said, "I've got tenure."

And Rickey said, "I've got 17-year."

Often, when Rickey would come up to bat with runners in scoring position, Padres third-base coach Tim Flannery would call "time" and walk down the baseline to meet him outside the batter's box.

For a very good reason: Whatever team Rickey happened to be with, and he was with nine during his career, some more than once, he had a problem remembering the signs.

The problem was, he didn't know them.

Flan would have to put his hands on Rickey's shoulders, look him straight in the eye and tell him exactly what he wanted him to do – bunt, hit away, take a pitch, whatever.

Otherwise, Rickey wouldn't have a clue.

———⊗⊗⊗———

When Rickey played for the Mets, he was asked where he was living in New York. He said: "Hey, I can open my drapes and see the *Entire* State Building."

———⊗⊗⊗———

Before the start of the 1982 season, Rickey got a $1 million signing bonus from the Oakland Athletics.

Some four months later, the team's accounting department noticed that the books weren't balanced.

Frantic, the bean counters discovered that Rickey's bonus check hadn't been cashed.

When the comptroller called Rickey and asked if he had cashed the check, he said, no, it was framed and hanging in his den.

"But what about the interest?"

"The what?"

———⊗⊗⊗———

When I first met Andy Strasberg, he had been with the Padres in various roles for several years.

Our conversation went something like this:

Me: "You're from the Bronx?"

Andy: "Yeah, I went to PS 105."

Me: "Son of a gun. Me, too."

Turns out we went to the same school at the same time – one year apart.

Old home week.

Andy was – still is – a very creative guy who developed a lot of promotions and products that are now widely used by all major-league teams to attract fans.

As Andy would tell you, it's much easier when your team is good, and a whole lot harder when your team isn't.

It was Andy who hatched The Chicken. It was Andy who designed MLB's first All-Star Game logo. It was Andy who first opened All-Star Game practices to the public.

So much more.

But there's something even more amazing about Andy that goes beyond his promotional ideas.

Remember the scene in *Annie Hall* where Woody Allen and Diane Keaton are in the movie line and two eggheads behind him are debating philosopher Marshall McLuhan's theories on communication?

Allen steps out of the line and brings McLuhan himself to confront these two guys. Then, McLuhan, who wrote *The Medium is the Massage*, says, "You don't know *anything* about my work."

We'd all kill for an "in your face" moment like that.

So, who goes to Yankee Stadium as a baseball-loving kid, sits in the right-field stands and strikes up what turned out to be a life-long friendship with the great Roger Maris?

Andy Strasberg.

Who introduced me to Yogi Berra and so many other former Yanks of my youth? Andy.

Now let's fast forward to Andy's college days.

His idol Maris has been traded to St. Louis and is coming to play the Pirates. He tells his buddies, "Let's go to the game. Roger Maris is a friend of mine."

As you'd expect, the response is, "Yeah, right, you know Maris? The guy who broke Babe Ruth's 60 home-run record for a season? Yeah, sure, you do."

Fast forward to Forbes Field in Pittsburgh. Andy and his guys are out in the right field bleachers as Maris jogs out to shag balls before the game.

He looks in the stands and yells, "Andy Strasberg! What are you doing in Pittsburgh?"

I love that story.

That's Andy.

Who, of course, agrees with me to this day that Roger Maris is the *true* single-season home-run hitter in baseball history.

Not Barry Bonds. Period. End of story.

Denny Matthews, longtime voice of the Kansas City Royals, was doing a drop-in for Guy's Potato Chips, which had recently added peanuts to their lineup.

As he read the drop-in, he decided to ad-lib, saying, "And ladies, while you're there, grab some Guy's nuts!"

He proudly told that story in his Hall of Fame induction speech.

Bob Uecker, voice of the Milwaukee Brewers and another Hall of Fame broadcaster, recalled his first Major League game as a player back in 1962.

Born and raised in Milwaukee, he had his parents and all his relatives in the stands, eager for him to make his debut.

"As I'm on the field," he said, "everybody was pointing at me and waving and laughing."

That's when his manager, Birdie Tebbetts, came up and asked him if he was nervous.

"No, because I've been waiting five years to get here," said Uecker. "I'm ready to go."

"Well, that's great, you're in the starting lineup," said Tebbetts. "But, by the way, the rest of us up here wear that supporter on the *inside*."

29

Gut-churning turbulence

"You keep talkin' like that, they're gonna cancel."

ONE TIME, BACK IN THE MID-1990S, Jerry Coleman and I rented a car in Fort Lauderdale when the Padres were playing the Marlins.

Even though the games were in Miami, about a half-hour or so away, we stayed in Fort Lauderdale in those early years of the Marlins franchise.

Dick Freeman, who was then the Padres' president, insisted that when we were on the road that I'd be the one who would rent the car and serve as Jerry's driver, back and forth from the stadium and wherever we were staying.

Out of respect for Jerry's age, he didn't want him to be forced to wait an hour or so after each game for the team bus.

This time, I rented a Budget rent-a-car and it was a lemon, at least the tires were. After the game, I was driving us back to the hotel when one of our tires blew out.

Somehow, driving on a flat tire, we were able to make it back to the Budget office close to our hotel. Trouble was, the jerk behind the desk wanted me to personally pay to replace the blown-out tire. I couldn't believe it.

I said, "Hey, *you* put the tire on. I didn't do anything to cause that tire to explode."

But Budget wouldn't budge, so I went ahead and paid for the tire.

I said to myself, "Oh, I'll get 'em tomorrow morning. Don't worry, they'll be sorry."

The next morning, I went on H&B and I started ranting about how I had rented a lemon from Budget and how they made me pay for the blown-out tire. So far, so good. We're all laughing because it made for a great story.

Only problem was, I forgot that KFMB had a long-running contract with Budget Car Sales as a morning-show sponsor – not Budget Rent a Car, but Budget Car Sales, part of the same company.

So, I'm just ripping Budget up and down, just having a great time.

After my segment, KFMB Radio general manager Paul Palmer called me into his office, and said, "You keep talkin' like that, they're gonna cancel. So, do me a favor. CUT IT OUT!"

I told him I would.

A few days later, still on the road, I got jerked around at the airlines check-in desk and because of that, barely made my cross-country flight.

The flight itself was awful, with gut-turning turbulence almost the entire way.

The next morning, I'm going on and on about how terrible the flight was, and Mac says, "What airline?"

"Well, Mac, I don't really want to say it on the air. I'm

already in trouble for something I said this week. Don't get me in trouble again."

Probably knowing that I couldn't *not* tell him what airline it was, Mac paused for a few seconds.

So, I went on: "But I'll tell you, on that flight, they served a *CONTINENTAL* breakfast and it's an airline that flies within the *CONTINENTAL* United States."

Right after that, Paul called me into his office again and said, "Dammit, Ted, we just had this conversation!"

"OK, Paul, I promise. Never again. I promise."

As I'm walking out, he says, "Ted?"

"Yeah?"

"You know, when you die, they're gonna have to *hire* pallbearers."

And I used that line at his memorial service, years later.

Instead of having a casket with pallbearers, they walked his ashes down the aisle. As a guest speaker at the reception afterward, I had that pallbearer line in my mind and I couldn't shake it.

So, I went ahead and shared Paul's zinger.

Thank God, they laughed.

Later, one of Paul's young grandsons came up to speak to me and said, "You know, Pop-pop would pick us up and we'd always do something fun. It was like going on a train. You knew you were going to have fun, but you had no idea where that train was going."

I love that one.

Just ask anyone who worked at KFMB Radio during the time he was there – he was in charge of both the AM and FM stations for more than 20 years – and they'll all tell you the same thing: Everyone loved Paul Palmer.

When Paul was still alive, we got together for lunch one day in late 2019.

Joining us were Andy Strasberg; Ted Giannoulas, otherwise known as The Famous Chicken; and Ballard Smith, the former Padres' president.

We had a great time, going over so many stories from those years. What a ride it was.

As I was driving home, Paul texted me and said, "Hey, you know what? I've never told you how great you were for us, generating the revenue you did and the ratings you helped us get. And I've never thanked you for that."

I texted him back: "Paul, when Jerry became the Padres manager in 1980, you helped me get Padres' play-by-play. You and Ballard could've gone with someone else, but you convinced the Padres that I was the right guy."

I continued: "Then you gave me the 7:15 and 8:15 morning sports on H&B, which became a huge success. And you gave me San Diego State football and basketball."

Then I added: "Paul, you don't owe me anything. I owe *you* everything for what my radio career has been, plus the talk shows and everything else. It's all been because of you."

I'm so glad I told him that because not more than a few weeks after our lunch, Paul Palmer died in a car crash.

30

Their saws are buzzing away

"They come in, no fuss, no muss, no noise."

THERE WERE SO MANY WONDERFUL MOMENTS when Jerry and I did what they call "drop-ins" during the broadcast, a series of "live" 20-second commercials.

When dot coms became prevalent, Jerry really had a hard time, as I do, with hi-tech. He finished one commercial by saying, "You can reach them anytime at www.com."

Over the years, he did quite a few for San Diego's Charco Construction, one of our most loyal sponsors.

One time, instead of doing a drop-in, it was a pre-recorded commercial.

In that commercial, unbeknownst to us, Jerry extolls the virtues of Charco, saying, "They're the best. They come in, no fuss, no muss. They clean up after themselves. You hardly know they're there. The best. I recommend Charco Construction."

Because both of us had taken off our headsets, we didn't hear the commercial, not a word of it.

When we came back on, just coincidentally, I said to Jerry, "You look kind of tired. You feeling OK?"

He said, "Well, the truth is, I'm tired because we're remodeling our home right now and there's crap everywhere. The noise is awful, their saws are buzzing away, going all the time.

"Maggie and I are living out in the garage while they're in the house doing the remodeling and it's driving us crazy.

"*That's* why I'm so tired."

Without realizing that his Charco commercial had just aired, he ripped Charco a new one.

Another magic moment.

When we were doing a game, one of the TV monitors in front of us was showing a Burger King commercial, with no sound, of course.

Maybe you've seen it, the one where this guy is dressed up as a king, wearing a crown and flowing cape, and his image is realistically transposed into an NFL Films highlight clip, so it looks very close to real.

There were several versions, but in this one, he's a defensive back who's on the field during an NFL game. He jumps in front of a receiver for an interception and scores a touchdown.

We came back from a break and Jerry, thinking it was a real NFL game, said on the air that he couldn't believe what he had just seen.

"You know what?" he said, "I was just watching the TV out of the corner of my eye here. And this is something I've wanted to say for a long time. These lunatics that go onto the field and disrupt the game..."

His voice rising in anger, he continued: "I'm telling you,

they oughta take those people and put 'em in jail, throw away the key, and keep 'em in jail!"

Right away, I turned my mic off because I couldn't stop laughing. Our longtime engineer, Dave Marcus, was turning so red from cracking up that I thought he might pass out.

After a few seconds of dead air, I decided I should tell Jerry what he had just seen.

"Jer, you know that guy running on the field? That was a Burger King commercial."

"Oh."

When we were in Cleveland, we had to put up with that crazy fan who dresses up as an Indian chief, wearing a full headdress and constantly banging a huge drum, non-stop.

It was driving both of us nuts.

At one point, the guy was banging his drum in the stands right below us. Jerry peered down at him and said to me on the air, "Who *is* that guy?"

I told him: "Jerry, that's the famous drummer who caused that big brouhaha because the Indians' front office wanted to kick him out. They got so many complaints from elderly fans that the Indians revoked his season ticket. But he went to court and forced the team to give them back."

"Don't you remember hearing that story?"

"No, I have no idea what you're talking about."

"Well, they went to court and the judge ruled that he could enter the stadium if he had a ticket, and that he needed to purchase another ticket for his drum. So, he's back here, banging his drum.

"That's the story."

Then Jerry said, "Well, why doesn't he go home and bang someone else?"

Right away, we went to a commercial and I said, "Jerry, did you hear what you just said?"

"What?"

"You said this guy should go home and bang someone else."

"No, I didn't. I said, 'Why doesn't he go bang some*thing* else."

So, I said to our producer, "OK, Dave, tell the studio to re-run the tape and play it for Jerry in his headset during the next break."

Dave racked it up for Jerry, who put on his headset. He heard what he had said, then calmly took his headset off, looked at me and said, sheepishly, "Well, I guess I did say that."

And Jerry and I both just lost it.

Then I said, "Don't worry, you're Jerry Coleman. There'll be no repercussions whatsoever."

And there weren't.

31

Nah, don't bother

*"By the time the game was over,
I thought I'd gone deaf."*

JUST AS I'VE WORN GLASSES almost my entire life, I'm not ashamed to say that I've worn hearing aids for quite a few years now.

Losing your hearing isn't all that uncommon for people like me who spend so much time wearing headsets, with mine cranked up to high volume because I like to hear my voice as opposed to crowd noise.

I'm certain that the first time I became aware I was losing my hearing dates back to a San Diego State basketball game that I did in Lawrence, Kansas, when the Aztecs played Kansas, on January 5, 2014, a date I'll always remember – for more than one reason.

The Aztecs, led by Skylar Spencer, who vastly out-played now NBA All-Star Joel Embiid of the 76ers, beat Kansas, 61–57.

That ended the Jayhawks' 68-game non-conference winning

streak at Allen Fieldhouse, named for legendary coach Phog Allen.

During the game, I got wrapped up in the flow and didn't lower the volume in my headset.

Big mistake.

I've never heard a louder basketball crowd than I heard that afternoon. It was unbelievable. Even my headphone controls couldn't dim the sound all that much.

By the time the game was over, I was hearing distortion like I'd never heard before and I was certain I'd gone at least partially deaf.

Then came the real shocker.

Moments later, as I was about to do the post-game interview with Aztecs coach Steve Fisher, I wasn't prepared for what came next.

My engineer said, "Pick up the phone. They want to talk to you back at the studio."

That's when I heard, "Do you want to make the announcement? We think you should be the one who makes it."

"What announcement? What are you talking about?"

"Jerry Coleman died tonight."

Hearing those words, I couldn't even think. It was inconceivable to me that Jerry was gone.

Earlier that day, I had called Jerry's wife, Maggie, when I got to Lawrence to ask how he was doing, and she sounded fairly optimistic. At least that's what I remember.

After talking to Maggie, I thought, "He's such a tough Marine, there's no way he won't make it. Two wars couldn't kill him, so that fall he took the other day won't kill him. He's going to be just fine," which was exactly what had I told myself after Jerry and I talked a few days before.

That's when he was in the hospital and I called to say, "Hey, Jer, I'm comin' to see you."

"Nah, don't bother," he said, sounding upbeat. "I'm out of here. I'll see you later."

When I asked Jerry what was going to happen next, he said, "Oh, they're trying to get me in a wheelchair down to the door to get me out of here, but that's ridiculous. I don't need a wheelchair."

He sounded great, which lifted my spirits.

I never saw him or talked to him again.

For the post-game show, I started by saying, "I have to make an announcement to you that Jerry Coleman died tonight."

I said, "Jerry was my friend, my mentor, my brother ... this Yankee, this Padre, this warrior for his country..."

All I could add was: "There are no words. There are just no words. If there are, I certainly don't have them. I don't know what to say to you, but I do know the love he had in this community that no broadcaster ever had, or will ever have."

It was awful. I was so upset I could hardly breathe.

Now, we were headed to the airport and I noticed that I couldn't hear what anyone was saying.

Instead of hearing their voices, what I heard was a distorted version of what they were saying.

All these fans who had flown to Lawrence for the game came up to me to tell me how sorry they were that Jerry had passed – except I couldn't make out what they were trying to tell me.

Then Aztecs coach Steve Fisher and assistant coach Brian Dutcher came up to me to express their condolences, and

I couldn't hear them very well either. Trying to stay calm, I thought, "Uh-oh, something's *very* wrong."

Up until that point in my life, I hadn't noticed any significant loss of hearing, not ever.

Looking back, I'm not exactly sure how much lasting damage I did to my hearing that day, but it had to be significant.

When I got back to San Diego, I took an auditory test that verified my worst fears.

My hearing was half-gone in one ear and not quite that much in the other, so I got outfitted with hearing aids. They're kind of a hassle, and an affront to my vanity, but I can hear much, much better and I'm grateful.

That Kansas game – which I'm convinced was the greatest Aztecs' win of all time – was also, in terms of learning about Jerry's passing, one of the worst moments of my life.

From the highest of highs in my professional career to the lowest of lows in my personal life, all within a matter of 30 seconds.

32

Toy phones

"Did one of you guys knock the phone off the hook?"

ONE OF MY FAVORITE HUDSON & BAUER stories had nothing to do with something I said on the air.

Instead, it had to do with something that happened when I was doing the show. Early one morning, two cops came to our Scripps Ranch home where I was living at the time.

I was on-air, yukking it up with H&B on the 8:15 segment as I reclined in my office studio, talking into my desk microphone, comfortably still attired in my undies.

Maybe the cops were expecting to see someone tied up with a gag in his mouth, but no, there was only Uncle Teddy, in his undies, talking on the radio, as if that was nothing out of the ordinary, which it wasn't for me.

I was almost done with what H&B named "Ted's Harangue," either mini or maxi, which became a daily feature, when I looked out the window.

I couldn't believe my eyes.

These two San Diego County sheriff deputies were staring

through the window and into my office, and one actually had his pistol drawn. I thought to myself, I know some of my listeners don't like me, but this is going *way* too far.

As quickly as possible, without letting our listeners know something out of the ordinary was going on, I wrapped up my segment.

Still not having the slightest idea why the deputies were there, I waved to indicate that I'd meet them at the front door.

Our twin boys, Nick and Ryan, who were about a year-and-a-half at the time, loved to play with our phones wherever they found one. We bought them their own toy phones, which, of course, they didn't like nearly as much as the real thing.

Unbeknownst to me, they had knocked our main house phone off the hook and then started pushing the digits, having no clue what they were doing.

One of them – we never figured out which one – must've pushed 9, then 1, and 1. Then they must've heard something like, "9-1-1 operator, how may I help you?"

But since they were little kids and could only speak – to paraphrase Mel Brooks in *Blazing Saddles* – authentic toddler gibberish, they didn't say anything.

Of course, that 9-1-1 operator must've thought that it was a call from a desperate hostage who couldn't speak.

Whatever, the operator looked at the screen, saw my address and dispatched these two very serious-looking deputies to our home. When "Leitner residence" came up, they recognized my name.

After I signed off with H&B, I quickly put on a pair of pants and went to the front door. I still didn't have any idea why they were there, but after they explained how they got the call, we tried to put the pieces together.

I said, "Well, I'm fine, so are my wife and kids."

We invited them into the house and as we walked back into our bedroom, there was the evidence – the main house phone lying on the floor. And I said something like, "You don't suppose…"

One of the deputies said, "All we know is that someone who lives in this residence dialed 9-1-1, either on purpose or by accident."

The twins were right beside us, listening, so I asked one of them, "Did you knock the phone off the hook?"

With his best "Who me?" expression, he pointed to his brother. Being the top-notch interviewer that I am, I asked the other one, "Did you dial it?"

And he pointed to his brother.

Having impeccable detective skills, the deputies quickly surmised that one of the twins had hit 9-1-1 by accident. We just shook our heads and had a good laugh about it.

What a morning *that* was.

And what a wonderful story I had for H&B the next day.

Back in the 1980s, when the Giants still played in Candlestick Park, I happened to notice a newspaper article that was prominently posted on the visitor's clubhouse bulletin board.

It was about a man whose most important body part fell off because – and this isn't so funny – he had repeatedly injected cocaine into his most private part.

I figured the article would be a provocative topic for my next morning's H&B segment.

I started by saying, "You know, guys, there's an article in yesterday's *San Francisco Chronicle*" – and I told the story. We were laughing like school kids, then Mac said, "I mean, can you *imagine* if it just fell off?"

Thank you, Mac...

"Yep, I can just picture it, this guy in the bathtub reaching for the washcloth or his rubber ducky, and now all of a sudden, he sees something floating in the bathwater and says, 'Aw, man, c'mon, it's already been a bad day.'

"I *need* that thing!"

We couldn't stop laughing.

Hey, there's a little boy in each of us and that was about as great an H&B moment as we ever had.

WE'LL BE RIGHT BACK
AFTER THESE WORDS

PART 8

"Hey, Goose, let me ask you a question."

Quite a few years ago, for one of the Yankees' Old Timers' Games, Billy Crystal was hired to serve as MC, a perfect gig for Billy, who grew up absolutely adoring the Yankees.

In the team's official prepared script, Billy was supposed to introduce Joe DiMaggio, at his insistence, with the words, "The world's greatest living ballplayer."

This was well before Mickey Mantle, Billy's childhood idol, had passed on.

Billy worshiped the grass that Mickey walked on, so there was no way he could read that line in good conscience – not in front of 60,000 fans at Yankee Stadium.

Instead, Billy introduced DiMaggio as "the great Yankee Clipper ... Joltin' Joe DiMaggio!"

Afterward, at a team VIP event, Billy said DiMaggio came up to him and said in an agitated voice, "That's the *world's greatest living ballplayer!*"

Then he punched Billy in the stomach, hard, doubling him over.

Not a flattering story for the great Joe DiMaggio, but not surprising.

Jerry Coleman once told me – and he had a good relationship with Joe – that if you ever mentioned his wife Marilyn Monroe in DiMaggio's presence or even asked about her, he wouldn't talk to you ever again.

In his eyes, teammate or not, you were done.

———— ✕✕✕ ————

In the early 2000s, the Houston Astros had a coach named Matt Galante, who stood 5-foot-6, and didn't mind guys making fun of his height.

One of the Astros players, Casey Candaele, took one of those small, three-pronged plastic pieces that Italian restaurants put in pizza boxes and made a big ceremony out of placing it on the floor of the clubhouse.

He put a towel around his forearm like a maître d' and announced with a flourish, "Galante, table for one."

———— ✕✕✕ ————

Goose Gossage, who spent a few productive seasons with the Padres in the 1980s, was a fearsome sight with his Fu Manchu and constant scowl.

But when he first joined the Yankees in 1978, he blew a few early-season save situations.

During that stretch, as he was being driven from the bullpen by car and into another relief situation, Yankees outfielder Mickey Rivers jumped onto the hood of the car, spread-eagled, yelling, "No! no, anybody but Goose!"

———— ✕✕✕ ————

This is the same Mickey Rivers whose nickname was "Chance" because his teammates thought he was the least likely ever to be chancellor of a university.

But this was Rivers' response after teammate Reggie Jackson claimed he had an IQ of 160.

"What, out of a thousand?"

Reggie then told Mickey, in front of the New York writers,

who ate up their byplay, that he should spend more time learning how to read and write.

Mickey's retort: "You'd better stop readin' and writin' and start hittin'!"

And there's no doubt that Mickey had Reginald Martinez Jackson pegged when he told him, "No wonder you're all mixed up. You got a white man's first name, a Spanish man's second name, and a black man's third name."

San Diego's Graig Nettles, another ex-Yankee who spent valuable time with the 1980s Padres, was good friends with Gossage, going back to their Yankees days.

So much so that Nettles, during a mound visit with two runners on base and a 3–0 count, asked Goose, who was having trouble throwing strikes, "Hey, Goose, let me ask you a question."

"What do *you* want?"

"Do they have a home plate in the bullpen?"

Only Nettles, with his sharp-edged wit, could've gotten away with a line like that to Goose.

Rivers, who was a terrific center-fielder, had one game where he cracked up Yankees pitcher Catfish Hunter, who was getting lit up.

Mickey was running all over the place, banging up against the wall, making great catches and a couple he couldn't get to.

When he got back to the dugout, he put on the catcher's chest protector backward, so that his back was protected.

As he ran out to this position, Catfish saw him and went down to one knee, he was laughing so hard.

That was Mickey.

I felt privileged to take part in the 2012 Petco Park ceremony to honor my friend, Colonel Coleman.

33

On each other's nerves

"Hey, what're you doing in my seat?"

AS THE CLICHÉ GOES, baseball's a funny game.

Baseball players like to joke around, get on each other's nerves, and, more than any other sport I've been around, they like to laugh with each other and *at* each other – a lot.

Some of the things I've seen over the years have been hilarious.

Again, let's take Rickey Henderson, who had two stints with the Padres (1996–1997), and then again in 2001. He existed in a world all his own and no one else came close.

One time, Rickey was on third, with Ryan Klesko at the plate. Rickey shouted to Klesko, "C'mon, T, drive me in."

Let me repeat: The batter was Ryan Klesko, not Tony Gwynn.

Surely, Rickey knew that "T" was Tony Gwynn's nickname, but Klesko later told me that half the time he had no idea what Rickey was talking about.

Whether Rickey knew the names, even the nicknames, of his teammates, I'm not too sure. Neither was Rickey.

But Rickey was the greatest lead-off hitter of all time, a true first-ballot Hall of Famer. As Rickey might say about himself, Rickey could play.

In 2001, the second of his two Padres stints, he set major-league records with career walks (2,062), career runs scored (2,245) and he also collected his 3,000[th] career hit on the final day of the season.

Impressive.

It was reported that Rickey, who didn't want to overshadow Tony Gwynn's final game after his amazing 20-year Padres career, offered to sit out that season-ending game.

As Tony later said, Rickey told him: "Rickey needs to let you enjoy your last game in the big leagues."

But Tony talked him out of not playing, a good move for both.

A sellout crowd of 60,000 showed up that day at Qualcomm Stadium to wish Tony farewell, and both Tony and Rickey got into the record books.

Rickey also impressed me in another way when I shared a flight with him to Oakland in early July 2009, me to do a Padres game and Rickey headed back to his hometown.

He told me he'd been auditing a speech class at an East Bay college, to help him get better prepared for his Hall of Fame induction speech, which was coming up in a few weeks.

That convinced me, as if any convincing was needed, that Rickey was a true pro.

Kevin Mitchell, a San Diego native who played for the Padres in 1987, was also "different" – with talent to spare.

One time, we were trying to leave Montreal airport before it got shut down by the curfew, but there was a problem.

We were getting on board and almost ready to roll, but Mitchell was stuck in customs, trying to get the inspector to approve his carry-on bag without paying Canada's duty tax.

So, John "Doc" Mattei, our longtime traveling secretary, a gruff-talking cigar-smoker and one-time podiatrist, came up to Mitch and said, "What's going on here?"

Mitch told Doc that he had bought his new sports jackets the last time the Padres were in Montreal a while back, and that he'd already paid the duty tax.

"And I ain't payin' it again," he said. "This is total BS."

The inspector opened the bag and saw that Mitch's sports jackets still had the price tag, because, of course, he *had* just bought them on this trip.

Doc proceeded to take out a big roll of $100 bills that he always carried and paid the inspector. Then he grabbed Mitch by the shoulder and said, "C'mon, let's get out of here."

We did, but just barely.

On another trip to Montreal, the Padres' charter flight arrived late at night in and we had to take a long bus ride to get our hotel.

Right away, the driver got lost. He had no idea where we were or where we needed to go.

It was already 2 in the morning. We were driving in this quiet residential neighborhood and the players were getting all over the driver's ass, "Come on, bussy, where the hell you takin' us?"

By now, we were driving along a narrow street when we accidentally rammed into a parked car where, believe it or not, this couple was naked inside, making love in the back seat.

Of course, the players were all awake, staring in amazement

at what we were all seeing. This poor guy was trying to get dressed and his lady friend was trying to do the same.

You can't make this stuff up.

———— ∞ ————

Yet again in Montreal, our bus driver got very lost.

After getting ragged by the players, he figured it was time to ask someone, anyone, for directions.

He stopped the bus at a street corner and asked a teenager who happened to be standing there if he'd give us directions to the Sheraton Hotel.

That's when one of the players said, "Hey, kid, why don't you get on the bus and take us there?"

So, the kid climbed the stairs and told the driver how to get to the Sheraton. Sure enough, we got there.

As we were getting off, the players started handing him $100 bills, peeling off one after the other.

Earlier, they'd all been paid their per-diem meal money and, as a result, that kid walked away with several thousand dollars in tips.

We made it to our hotel, and that kid made out like a bandit.

34

Sitting in my big recliner

"I couldn't believe you were still talking."

I HAD MY OWN STYLE because I didn't want to be like anyone else.

Early in my career, though, I was influenced by several broadcasters and even took on some of their techniques before I fully developed my own.

My Padres on-air partners – Jerry Coleman, Bob Chandler and Dave Campbell – each taught me the game of baseball from the inside out.

Until I became part of the Padres' radio team in 1980, I was strictly a football and basketball guy. And until you actually do major-league play-by-play, you're not a baseball guy.

I worked alongside two former major-leaguers in Jerry and Dave – along with Bob, whom I used to call "BCPC," as in my personal computer, because he had about as much knowledge about the game as anybody.

I learned a lot about the art and science of calling baseball from those guys, including Jerry's cardinal rule you should never, *ever* correct your partner's mistakes on the air.

When mistakes did happen, and I'm sure I made plenty, they'd let me know either by a quick written note or by a quick conversation during commercial breaks.

Believe me, they could've thrown me under the bus numerous times, but the Colonel had taught them, and me, that you never make your partner look bad. You always promote him and support him, no matter what.

Thank you, Jerry, Bob, and Dave.

Even years later, when I thought I knew baseball very well, trust me, I still learned a ton of new things from my partners Tim Flannery and Bob Scanlan.

OK, I realize I said earlier that I developed my own style. That's true, because when I got started in the business, I didn't have squat for style.

Let's just say that I was "greatly influenced" by a few favorite radio broadcasters of my childhood.

My No. 1 influence would be Marty Glickman, whom I listened to growing up as the radio voice of the NFL's New York Giants and the NBA's New York Knicks.

For my first few years of doing football and basketball play-by-play at Oklahoma State and Oklahoma, I was, basically, being *Teddy* Glickman. I relied on his phraseology and techniques because that's all I knew.

In case you haven't heard of Glickman, he was a wonderful broadcaster who literally came up with the original basketball terms of "the lane" and "top of the key" and "the midcourt stripe" and many others, even "Swish!" for a perfect shot.

That was all Marty Glickman.

He was also an incredible track athlete who made the 1936 US Olympic team that went to Berlin. But he never got to run.

The US track coach, along with US Olympic president Avery Brundage, a noted anti-Semite, didn't want to risk insulting Hitler any more than necessary.

The legendary American sprinter Jesse Owens, who was Black, had already won three of his four gold medals.

Brundage didn't allow Glickman, who was Jewish, to run in the 400-meter relay. Another Jew on the relay team, Sam Stoller, was also pulled. Both runners were replaced by Black sprinters.

In 1985, Glickman went back to that stadium in Berlin and sat in Hitler's box. He leaned back and said to himself, "Well, I win. I'm here and you're not."

Going back 20 years or so, when I started my early home-run call of "Ball going, ball gone!" that was supposed to be my personal tribute to Mel Allen, who did the Yankees' broadcasts when I was a kid.

In terms of influence, not technique but opinion and commentary, I always admired the once-and-always-great Howard Cosell. No one did what he did.

Like him or not, he was an original who dared to spout his opinions over the air, in a far more innocent era when newspaper writers like Dick Young, Cosell's print nemesis, did that.

I was always fascinated that the hardcore newspaper guys like Young absolutely despised Cosell, when, in fact, he was just doing on TV and radio what they'd been doing in their papers for decades.

In Cosell's national prime, spanning the late 1960s and into much of the 1980s, there was nobody like him and probably never will be again.

He paved the way for guys like me, away from all those

ex-jocks and hacks who had no business being in the booth because they had nothing worthwhile to say.

Cosell once said of himself: "I've been called arrogant, pompous, obnoxious, vain, cruel, verbose, a showoff. I am, of course, all of those things."

Yes, he was all of those things, but what Cosell did for sports and broadcasting changed both forever, and for the better.

———— ⬤⬤ ————

When I joined Channel 8 in 1978, I started saying "My Padres" when they won, and "Your Padres" when they lost, which up-set a lot of viewers because they wanted me to be a homer and openly root for the Padres.

That wasn't my style, and besides, during those years, they lost a lot more games than they won.

When I became a Padres' play-by-play voice in 1980, I didn't bring "My Padres" and "Your Padres" with me because that was a different on-air role and I was now a team employee.

But I continued saying it on Channel 8, and like a lot of what I used to do on TV, our viewers either loved it or hated it.

Same thing with "Who cares?" – because I didn't.

During the past 10 years or so, I started saying at the end of a Padres win, "THIS GAME BELONGS TO MY SAN DIEGO PADRES!" – which made everyone happy.

About 10 years ago, I accidentally came up with, "THAT BALL WAS CAA-RRUUSHED!" for a Padres home run.

That first came out of my mouth as "That ball wasn't just crushed, it was "CAA-RRUUSHED!" That's when I thought to myself, "Wow, that sounded pretty good."

I wish I would've come up with that line a lot sooner because that's how fans started to greet me around town. They'd say, "Hey, Uncle Teddy, THAT BALL WAS CAA-RRUUSHED!"

I loved that and I miss it.

When I was working in Hartford, the station's lead anchor was a fellow whose colleagues didn't care for. Whatever his name was, his wife's nickname was Chipper.

One time, I was out sick with the flu for a few days and then I came back. On-air, he said to me, "It's good to have you back, Ted. How you feeling?"

My reply was, "Well, I'm not exactly feeling chipper, but I'm OK."

The studio cameraman, a tough old union guy, laughed so hard that he fell to one knee behind his camera. I can see him now with his hand over his face, he was laughing so hard.

He knew I had done that on purpose.

Then there was the time I got a call from a Hartford cop, who said he was a fan and watched me all the time.

He said, "I was sitting in my big recliner and I fell asleep watching you do the 6:20 sports. When I woke up, you were still on, so I assumed you were just wrapping up the sports."

"I thought I had taken a short nap, but I looked out the window and it was dark. I couldn't figure what was going on. Then I realized that I'd slept like a baby for five hours and when I woke up at 11:25, you were still doing the sports.

"I couldn't believe you were still talking."

What else is new?

In the 1990s, a Hudson & Bauer listener named Jim came up with a song whose main lyric was that if you had a question, you should "ask ol' Ted."

Problem was, with his Southern accent, it sounded a lot like "A–hole Ted."

As Padres president/CEO Larry Lucchino liked to say, like anchovies, I was "an acquired taste."

35

My marriages

"They're the lucky ones, and I wasn't."

WHATEVER I WANT, I WANT IT NOW. That's who I am. Who knows, maybe that comes from my childhood where I was told no, no, no all the time by my father.

I'm impulsive, and whether it's buying a house, buying a car, or getting married, I always rush into things, often without thinking. I've been that way my entire life.

As for marriage, as so many of us know, *getting* married is the easy part, but staying married can be a challenge.

It's said that more than 50 percent of marriages end in divorce and the other half undoubtedly go through hard times, but somehow, they manage to stay together.

They're the lucky ones and I wasn't. Ultimately, it was my fault, with an exclamation point. Nobody forced me to get married.

Rather than get into specifics or say anything negative about the mothers of my children, I'd just like to say the following: Whatever happened between me and my former wives, that stays between us.

Now, boys and girls, let's move on, shall we?

Posing with the great Yogi Berra at the Hall of Fame induction ceremonies for Tony Gwynn, July 28, 2008.

36

Tony Gwynn, Part 4

"We know he's gonna get through this."

IN HIS FINAL YEAR OR SO, Tony Gwynn frequently mentioned to me, in his understated way, how perplexed he was that his doctors just couldn't nail "this thing" that was overtaking his body.

He really hated doing the radiation treatments, where he had to wear a net-like hood over his head when he underwent all those tests. The whole thing made him want to run away and hide.

He told me that several times he jumped off the examining table and started walking out of the exam room, and his wife Alicia had to coax him to come back

She'd say, "You know you've got to do this. Now *do* it."

She was his great mentor, his great coach, and his great wife in terms of making sure Tony did what he had to do.

Many times, while Tony was still doing the Padres' telecasts in the next booth, he'd come over during breaks to talk with Jerry and me.

That was after he had undergone the surgery that resulted in him having to talk out of the side of his mouth.

I'd have to turn my head because it broke my heart to see Tony that way. And I didn't want him to see that I was tearing up.

Tony's death, so young at 54, truly surprised me because a week or so before, I'd seen his son in Philadelphia when he was with the Phillies, and he had given me a surprisingly optimistic report.

Whether it was for public consumption or not, I didn't know, but I got excited when Tony Jr. said, "We know he's gonna get through this," and, "Don't worry, he's gonna be fine."

Based on that, I really didn't think Tony would die from what he had.

After talking to Tony Jr., I felt a little more positive for a few days and then we flew to New York for three games, then to Seattle for a four-game series.

That's when I had planned to go visit my kids who lived in nearby Olympia at the time. I was going to rent a car when we landed at SeaTac Airport, pick them up and bring them to Seattle, so we could be together for a couple of days.

On the morning of June 16, the phone rang and their mom said to me, "I don't know if you've heard, but Tony Gwynn died early today."

I was devastated, absolutely inconsolable.

I knew I couldn't let my kids see me like this, so their mom and I agreed that I wouldn't be picking them on this trip. She understood, and they understood, because they all knew how I felt about the great Tony Gwynn.

It was going to be hard enough for me to do that night's

game – and make the announcement about Tony's passing and react to it at the beginning of the broadcast. I knew I needed time to gather my emotions and my thoughts.

To this day, I don't remember exactly what I said, but I do know that I said something in the opening segment and then something else later in the game. I also knew it wasn't enough.

How could it be?

Whatever I said, it was heartfelt and painful. I had a lost a true friend and I still don't believe it.

There's a gravestone near my mother's grave that carries this inscription: "Those who live in hearts left behind will never die."

I'm convinced that with the love we all have for "T," for as long as we are here, Tony is here.

———⚬⚬⚬———

When Jerry Coleman left us, he was almost 90, so while it was a terrible loss, his passing wasn't as much of a shock to me as was losing Tony Gwynn.

Truth is, I never thought Jerry would die, at least not in the abstract sense.

But in reality, I knew it would happen, maybe when he got to be 95 or so because he had longevity in his family.

One time, we were running late to an event that Jerry and I were going to MC, which we did a lot in those days. But he kept talking on the phone.

After he finally hung up, I happened to ask him who he was talking to, and he said, "My older sister." And I thought, "I'm so glad she's alive because I'm now convinced that he *will* make 95."

Alas, it wasn't to be.

Same thing with Tony, because even though we all knew his health was failing, I had convinced myself that he would make a full recovery.

I didn't know what his true condition was or what his chances of recovery were. I just wasn't thinking in those terms, so when he died, it was both shocking and debilitating at the same time.

When I think of Tony, I can't help but think back to when the Padres played the Yankees in Game 1 of the '98 World Series at Yankee Stadium.

In the bottom of the 1st inning, I was watching him as he ran out to right field.

As he got to his position, Tony looked up to the sky.

After the game, I said to him, "I know what you were doing."

"When?"

"When you ran out there and looked up to the sky."

"Yeah, you're right. I was talking to my dad. He would've loved this so much."

Later, in 2004, a few hours before Tony was to give his Hall of Fame induction speech, he asked me, "Can we get together? I need to talk to you about something."

Surprisingly, he was nervous – who wouldn't be? – and wasn't sure how to mention his dad and keep his composure to finish his speech.

That's not unusual for a public speaker to have some trepidation when placed in a different role.

It's like the research that shows that most people's biggest fears are public speaking and dying.

Or as Jerry Seinfeld put it, "In essence, you'd rather be in the coffin than give the eulogy."

Tony went on: "You know what having my dad here would've meant to me. Everything. What should I do?"

I said, "It's easy, really. Don't mention any of the family stuff until the end. That's when you should say that your dad would've been absolutely beaming today. He would've loved this moment."

"OK, I'll do that."

And that's what he did.

Seven years later, he was gone.

When I think about those we've lost – Jerry Coleman, Tony Gwynn, Junior Seau, Dick Enberg – I still can't believe they're not with us anymore.

WE'LL BE RIGHT BACK AFTER THESE WORDS

PART 9

"It was my pleasure."

Back in 1982, when Steve Garvey joined the Padres, I was asked to speak to a women's realty group at the Lawrence Welk Resort in North County.

It was a hot August day and everyone was boiling, even in the meeting room. For some reason, the AC wasn't on.

I started by saying, "I know, I know, I don't get that many speaking requests anymore because Steve Garvey's now with the Padres, and everyone wants *him*, not me. Everyone loves Steve, which I can understand.

"He's a wonderful guy and a great player."

Later, I was sweating bullets because it was getting really hot in that room.

I said, "No offense, ladies, but you've rented this room and I realize that costs money. But maybe you could've paid a little more and turned on the air conditioning!"

Then this lady in the back of the room – she must've been at least 80 – with perfect timing shouted out, "We would've turned it on for Garvey!"

———— ⚭ ————

After Steve hit that amazing home run in Game 4 of the NLCS in 1984 that allowed the Padres to live another day and beat the Chicago Cubs, he uttered one of the more memorable quotes in Padres' history.

Moments after he crossed home plate, he was asked by ABC's Tim McCarver about his dramatic feat.

Like the hero he was, The Garv simply smiled and said, "It was my pleasure."

Later that night, when he walked into a swanky La Jolla restaurant, the entire place stood up and greeted him with a standing ovation.

———⊶⊷———

Longtime San Diego funnyman Russ T Nailz had a classic line about Uncle Teddy that got him laughs at the Comedy Store back in the 1980s.

He'd say: "You know, marketing research at Channel 8 shows that there are basically two kinds of people in San Diego. You either hate Ted Leitner. Or you *are* Ted Leitner."

———⊶⊷———

Kevin Mitchell, who played for the Padres in 1987, was one tough hombre.

How many other players do you know that would tell the entire pitching staff during spring training:

"Don't worry, if anyone charges the mound, I'll get there before they do. And I will kick their ass."

———⊶⊷———

As a huge fan of the Dodgers' legendary voice, Vin Scully – but aren't we all? – I'm pleased that he gets credit as the original source of one of baseball's more enduring truths.

In 1991, talking about the Chicago Cubs' Andre Dawson,

Vin said, "Andre has a bruised knee and is listed as day-to-day… (pause) But aren't we all."

Vin also liked to compare the overuse of statistics by broadcasters as being "Like the drunk leaning against the lamppost late at night. He's not doing it for illumination, but for support."

———— ⊗⊗⊗ ————

Back when Dan Fouts was with the Chargers, we'd do these Friday game-preview segments at Channel 8, usually in my office with us informally talking to each other.

One time, back when the Chargers and Padres were sharing Qualcomm Stadium, Fouts and I were taping the segment in the stands, not far from the field, when the Padres' Rollie Fingers looked up from the first-base dugout and saw us.

Then he yelled: "Hey, Dan, what're you talking to that bastard for?"

It wasn't easy being me.

———— ⊗⊗⊗ ————

About 10 years ago, my good friend John Sterling, the long-time voice of the New York Yankees, was on the team charter headed for Minneapolis in an extremely turbulent storm.

The players' air masks had deployed and things were getting scary.

John, who's known for his signature home-run call of, "*IT IS HIGH! IT IS FAR! IT IS GONE!*" told me he was oddly flattered by what happened next.

As things got even worse, a group of players began to mimic his home-run call by chanting, "*WE ARE HIGH! WE ARE FAR! WE ARE F---IN' GONE!*"

———— ⊗⊗⊗ ————

37

Smashed that pie

"Check under your seat for the little blue ticket."

DECEMBER 20, 1979 IS A DAY that shall live in infamy. Perhaps you were there. I know I was.

That night, I was the target of "Throw a Pie at Ted Leitner Night," a promotion held by the NBA's then-San Diego Clippers. At halftime of the Clippers' game against the New York Knicks, some 50 fans were chosen to toss a whipped-cream pie right in my face, one pie each per fan.

A few weeks earlier, I had agreed to be the featured victim, with the thought of "Sure, why not? What could it hurt?"

I'd only been at Channel 8 a short time and I'm sure that Bob Myers, GM of the KFMB stations, was wondering if this new guy who did the sports without a script – me – was generating ratings and whether he should pick up my option or not.

Or maybe he was thinking I'd be done after my first year.

At that night's Clippers game, a crowd of nearly 7,000 showed up, including those same rabid New York transplants who show up in droves when the Mets and the Yankees come to town to play the Padres.

Adjacent to one of the baskets, the setup was a thin wood sheet with an oval-shaped opening, just big enough for me to fit my truly big head in the middle.

Already revved up, the crowd was going nuts, even before the first pie took flight.

The PA announcer got things going by saying, "Check under your seat for the little blue ticket. If you have the blue ticket, you get to throw a pie at Ted Leitner's face!"

Trouble was, the Clippers' staff forgot – or hadn't bothered – to put a tarp or a cover on the court where this extravaganza was about to be held. Thinking back on the Clippers, let me add that, as usual, they had no clue.

By the way, why the hell were they throwing pies at *me*, instead of the team's clownish owner, Donald T. Sterling?

I got introduced by the PA announcer to a raucous mix of wild cheers and loud boos. I stuck my face into that opening and the "lucky" winners stood behind a line not more than a few feet away.

Then they took aim.

What I remember most is that Terrell Ward, a defensive back for the Aztecs, came up past the line, right up to me, and smashed his pie right into my face.

He hit me so hard that it was like being punched in the face.

The crowd went wild, and that was their favorite pie of the night.

When it was over, the playing surface under the basket was covered with mounds of cream pie remnants. There was so much that it took at least 40 minutes to get the mess off the floor.

On the bright side, Bob Myers told me later that it was the best pie-throwing contest he'd ever seen.

I wasn't so thrilled.

But professionally, that night was pivotal to my career because Bob later told me, "Whether they like you or not, they know you and obviously they've been watching you."

Bottom line: He picked up my option for the second year.

Look, Mom, I made the cover of San Diego Magazine *in October 1982, my first magazine cover and my last.*

38

My suitcase and my typewriter

"You told me to come back, didn't you?"

MY FIRST WEEK IN STILLWATER, Oklahoma, early September of 1965, there I was, a young teenager from New York with a heavy Bronx accent and totally out of my element.

The first on-campus event I went to at Oklahoma State was called, I kid you not, Howdy Week, or as it's known to the rest of the planet, Freshman Orientation.

This, at a school that once called itself "The Princeton of the Prairie."

Really?

That wasn't so fitting after Dexter Manley went to the Washington Redskins and they found that after four years at Oklahoma State, he couldn't read at all.

So much for Princeton.

Everyone was very friendly and welcomed me to town, even though most of them probably hadn't heard too many people talk like I did.

As in, *Tulser* for Tulsa, and *cawfee*, instead of coffee, and *New Yawk*. You get the idea.

Trying to venture out beyond the campus, I went down to Main Street and walked into a five-and-dime store called TG&Y that was very big in Oklahoma.

I picked up some school supplies and a soft drink, not much else, and after checkout, as I turned and started to walk out, the cute young clerk said to me, "Come back."

I thought what she wanted me to do was come back to the counter, as if I hadn't paid for everything or didn't get my change.

I turned around and said, "Yes?"

By that time, she was already starting to ring up the next person, but she looked up and saw me standing off to the side.

"Yes, sir?"

"You told me to come back, didn't you?"

"Oh, no. You're probably from out of town, right? Well, here in Oklahoma, we say, 'Come back,' or 'Y'all come back.' I was just saying thanks for coming in and come back again, y'hear?"

I started to laugh and thought, "Boy, do I feel stupid."

The customers waiting in line started to laugh, as well, at this dumb New York kid who had just arrived in town after a 39-hour bus ride with his suitcase and typewriter and not much knowledge about anything besides sports.

I went back to my dorm room, where my assigned room-mate, a football player from Tulsa, asked me if I wanted to go shopping downtown with him.

Except he didn't phrase it like that.

He said, "Let's go see what the Jews are selling."

Turns out, that's the expression they used to go shopping at the retail stores and the main department store, called Katz's.

Remember, this was 1965 in Oklahoma. You arrive and turn your watch back...to *1865*.

For example, one of my favorite TV commercials was for Mathis Brothers Furniture where a furniture store owner instead of giving the store hours, says, "We plow 9 to 9 on weekdays and 1 to 6 after church on Sunday. Y'all come see us, now hear?"

The late Larry King always said that discrimination, by its very nature, is just stupid, even silly. Over what? The shade and color of your skin? Your religious beliefs?

What nonsense. When you break it down like that, it's absurd — but not innocuous. It's self-esteem destroying, especially when it comes from people whom you consider your friends.

I remember sitting around with my buddies in grade school during lunch, which was held in the smelly old gym that was converted into the lunch room each day.

I liked all these guys, but they were bigots. We got to talking at lunch about our teacher and one of the friends brought up Mr. Gallagher, our eighth-grade homeroom science teacher.

"Oh, he's such a Jew," someone said.

Hearing my friend say that was like getting slapped in the face. All these guys knew I was Jewish. I felt like saying, "Hey, jerk, you want me to punch your face in?"

That's the way it made me feel.

I thought to myself, "What is it with these guys? I'm supposed to be their friend. What have I ever done to them? Why do people feel better by putting down others? Does that make 'em feel special?"

I'll never understand that and neither will anyone who's been made to feel so small.

When I was walking home from school with a friend of mine named Norman Bretel, I had to take a whiz like a racehorse.

So, I said, "Hey, Norm, can I go to the bathroom when we get to your house?"

"Sure."

Once we got there, he went up to his room and I headed to where I thought the bathroom was.

I said to his mother, who knew me from Cub Scouts, "Mrs. Bretel, may I please use your bathroom?"

And she said, "Oh, Teddy, we don't have a bathroom."

Since I was 8 years old, all I could say was, "OK, thank you, Mrs. Bretel."

Then I left and wet my pants on the way home, again like the proverbial racehorse.

When I got home, I quickly changed into another pair of pants. When my mom got home later that night, she was doing our laundry and said, "How come your pants in the bathroom are wet?"

After I told her the story, she gave me this pained expression, as if she understood exactly what was going on.

"She didn't want you to use the toilet because you're Jewish," she told me. "Some people are like that. And you're just going to have to deal with them."

She added, "Please don't tell your father. If he finds out, he'll go down there and start to curse and scream at them."

So, I didn't.

About 10 years later, in 1975, my father had a heart attack. He went to the hospital near my parents' apartment in Yonkers, New York, where I had grown up.

I drove to the hospital to visit him. We didn't hug in our family, so I just shook his hand as he was lying in bed, clearly in bad shape.

He took his oxygen mask off and said, "Guess who I saw here," and of course, I had no idea what he was going to say next.

"Who?"

"Mrs. Bretel. She's one of the assistants."

I started to laugh, and he said, "What?"

"Hey, good luck getting to the bathroom," I said.

"What do you mean?"

"Never mind, it's a long story."

Being Jewish, though I'm not at all religious, whenever I get asked if I've ever had to deal with discrimination, I say that I know what it sounds like, what it looks like and what it feels like.

Like I say, when I was growing up, I didn't have bullies pushing me against the wall and calling me a "dirty Jew" and punching me out, not like the kind of horror stories I've heard over the years from so many others.

Maybe it's because I knew how to make people laugh.

I've been lucky that way.

The many faces of Uncle Teddy.

39

Pretty much sank the franchise

"Little did I know where we both would be."

I NEVER SAW ANYONE PLAY BASKETBALL quite like Bill Walton, when he was at UCLA and later in the NBA when he was in the prime of his pro career.

Through my youth and calling as many college and pro games as I have, let me say without hesitation that Bill Walton was the greatest big man I've ever seen – when he was healthy.

I know some people will bring up Wilt and Kareem and Russell and Shaq and so many other all-time greats, but Bill was so different, with so many more skills – playmaking, scoring, passing, rebounding, overall court sense.

For me, no one was Bill's equal or could do *all* those things as well as he did. Not Wilt. Not Kareem. Not Shaq.

The first time I met Bill was in early 1977 when I was still in Philadelphia and he was in town with the Portland Trail Blazers. That morning, I went to the Blazers' shootaround and asked him if he could spare a few minutes for an interview.

He turned me down, perhaps because he was still

uncomfortable about his stuttering, which he eventually over-came, as we all know. Now he's one of the most recognized broadcasters anywhere, and as iconic a national sports figure as San Diego has ever known.

Little did I know where we both would be a year or so later. And it wasn't Philadelphia.

I wish I would've said, "Bill, I've looked at my crystal ball and it says that I'm going to go to your hometown to be on TV. And you'll be there, too."

In May of 1979, I kiddingly reminded Bill that he had turned me down.

That was the day of the press conference to announce that he had signed what was supposed to be a seven-year contract with the San Diego Clippers, who had moved from Buffalo a year earlier.

At nearly $7 million per year, Bill's deal made him the NBA's then-highest-paid player in history and a genuine national story, at least on the sports page.

I loved his quote when he was asked about his contract: "I'm making a living wage."

Pure Bill.

I thought, "This is going to be awesome. Not only is Bill Walton coming to town, but I'll be doing the play-by-play on Channel 8," which I did for several seasons.

Looking back, Walton's signing could've been as big of a hometown hero story as when "Aztec for life" Tony Gwynn was drafted by the Padres in 1981 and went on to become the legend he became.

But the Clippers' Walton Era was nothing but awful.

It was one injury after another for Bill and, as things turned out, the franchise was all but doomed.

Bill has undergone more than 35 surgeries in his life, which reminds me of one of his favorite lines, that "minor" surgery is surgery they perform on someone else.

In his inspiring 2016 book, *Back from the Dead*, he revealed that he was once in such unbearable pain that he seriously contemplated suicide. At one point, he was terribly distraught as he struggled to get into a therapy pool at the Mission Valley YMCA.

An older disabled veteran who happened to be walking by didn't recognize Bill but he did recognize the look of utter despair on his face.

He looked at Bill and said, "Don't do it."

"Do what?"

They both knew what they weren't saying.

Fortunately, his doctor was later able to perform successful spinal surgery, so that Bill could get back to being Bill Walton, this amazing athlete and living embodiment of what it takes to overcome pain and depression.

Bill now enjoys every moment of his life, riding his bike all over town, supporting every civic and charitable cause that's worth supporting, and espousing the glories of our San Diego lifestyle like no one else I've ever known.

———— ∞ ————

Of course, for the Clippers, not having Bill suit up for very many games turned out to be a moot point.

As many of us suspected would happen, team owner Donald T. Sterling moved the franchise to Los Angeles in May of 1984, under the cloak of darkness with a caravan of moving vans headed up Interstate 5.

What that man did to San Diego sports fans was disgraceful, matched only by what the Chargers did more than 30 years later.

Why does my beloved San Diego have to put up with all this crap from so many poorly run, failed franchises – the Rockets, the Conquistadors, the Sails, the Clippers, the Chargers...

Dammit, this is America's Finest City. Why didn't these sports owners treat us like something other than a bunch of small-market yahoos?

It pisses me off.

―――∞∞∞―――

You've got to admit there's never been any major sports franchise like the Clippers. And thank God for that.

One time, after a road trip, head coach Paul Silas came back to his office to find that one of the team's top executives had moved his stuff out and her stuff in.

The Clippers' media guide generously identified Patricia Simmons as assistant general manager, though as far as anyone could tell, she did absolutely nothing – except take over Silas' office and sit next to Sterling at home games.

That was the Clippers, a joke of a franchise except for a handful of players like Walton, Freeman Williams, Terry Cummings, Norm Nixon, Kermit Washington, World B. Free and Joe "Jelly Bean" Bryant.

When I was still in Philadelphia, I got to be friends with World (then known as Lloyd), and Joe when they were with the 76ers. Much later, of course, the world got to know Joe's son, the late Kobe Bryant, one of the game's all-time greats.

Don't forget, when we're talking about the Clippers, this was the team whose jackass owner ordered the trainer to re-use tape on the players' ankles to cut back on medical expenses.

Simply stunning. Typical Clippers.

———— ✕✕✕ ————

Paul Silas was a terrific guy who was saddled with less-than-terrific players. We got along great because he truly didn't care what I said about his coaching or the Clippers' usually dismal performances.

One time, I went on the 11 o'clock sports and ripped a few coaching moves he had made in that night's game, which I had broadcast on Channel 8.

The next day, I saw him and because I knew that he watched me all the time, I offhandedly said, "Hey, Paul, sorry about that comment."

Without missing a beat, he said, "Do you think I give a damn what you say?"

My kind of guy.

———— ✕✕✕ ————

Paul was preceded as the Clippers' coach by Gene Shue, who was a terrific NBA guard in his time, back in the 1950s and '60s.

You know the offensive spin move you see today's players make? A five-time NBA All-Star, Gene was the first to use it.

I had a great relationship with him, and I'm so happy he's hanging in there at almost 90 years of age.

Back when he was coaching the Clippers, and before charters, NBA teams flew commercial flights. All the available first-class seats were reserved for the more senior players – that is, those with the most years of service in the league.

Any remaining senior players sat back in coach, assigned three seats for every two players so they could spread out, only slightly more comfortably. That perk was guaranteed by their contracts.

So, there I was, sitting in coach when Coach Shue came and sat down next to me.

I said, "Geno, what the hell are you doing back here with lowly me and not in first-class?"

He explained the NBA's assigned-seat rule to me and shrugged his shoulders.

And I said, "After all these years, we find out that they call you 'Coach' because that's where you sit!"

He was less than amused.

40

Thrilled to be an Aztec

"How was the honeymoon?"

A LUCKY GUY?

Oh, puh-*leeze.*

From being born to an absolute angel through all the people who were there to help me or give me the multiple breaks I needed to be successful in broadcasting, lucky doesn't begin to describe how fortunate I've been.

Take the Aztecs' play-by-play job for football and basketball.

I'm still proud to be an Aztec and I love the loyalty they've shown me through the years.

On occasion, the Aztecs of old would change play-by-play broadcasters when they changed flagship radio stations.

The last time that happened, the new station wanted their guy to do the games, but former Aztecs athletic director Jeff Schemmel said, "No, we want Ted."

End of story.

Current AD John David Wicker has given me the same support. I've been so lucky that so many executives have had my back throughout my career.

As a point of interest, Jeff Schemmel's brother, Jerry, who's a good friend and a former voice of the Colorado Rockies, was on the DC-10 that crashed in an Iowa cornfield in 1989. He was one of 184 survivors, but more than 100 lives were lost in the crash.

Despite fire and smoke so thick he couldn't see his hand in front of his face, he got out safely.

Then he heard a baby crying and went back into the burning wreckage. He found the infant and her mom and carried them out to safety.

Jerry later wrote a book, *Chosen to Live*, about his experience and how he overcame survivor's guilt.

To this day, Jerry and that little girl, who's now in her 30s, still communicate with each other. And always will.

My association with the Aztecs and their coaches has been so cool, so rewarding, right up to the present-day with Brady Hoke and Brian Dutcher.

———— ∞ ————

My first Aztecs football coach was Claude Gilbert, a good guy who, like most football coaches, would answer a post-game question by saying, "I really won't know until I see the film."

At an Aztecs luncheon that I hosted each week in the 1980s, I was slightly late to the meeting because of a late flight on the way back from my honeymoon – don't be a wise-ass and say, "Which one?!" – and I rushed to the podium.

As I hurried past Coach Gilbert, he grabbed me and asked, "How was the honeymoon?"

I said, "I really won't know until I see the film."

I have, of course, since seen the film... And I was magnificent!

———— ∞ ————

At another one of those luncheons, the Aztecs were about to take on the then-monstrous Miami Hurricanes of the 1980s. We'd have a speaker phone on the table and I'd interview the opposing coach for the audience.

The 'Canes had Jimmy Johnson, whom I had covered when I was doing TV in Oklahoma City and he was head coach at Oklahoma State.

I hadn't talked to Jimmy in years but got him on the line, on speaker, without him knowing we had a live audience.

"Jimmy, Ted Leitner here with San Diego State. How've you been?"

"Ted Leitner? When the [bleep] did you get to San Diego?"

The crowd's laughter let a surprised Jimmy know that we were live.

Oops. Another magic Aztecs moment for Teddy.

Since I get asked all the time to choose my favorite Aztecs wins, I'd have to go with their 34–10 win over the University of Houston in the 2016 Las Vegas Bowl.

The night before the game at the team hotel, head coach Rocky Long told me, "We'll have trouble handling their team speed, but we'll adjust by halftime and kick their asses."

And that's exactly what happened.

It was an unbelievably exciting win against a great team that had upset Oklahoma earlier in the season.

As I was going down the press box elevator with ABC Sports' Brent Musburger, he said to me, "Hey, tell Rocky you guys really outplayed and out-coached those guys."

Later, on the team charter, message delivered.

Favorite basketball win?

No, it's not Kawhi Leonard, Billy White, Malcolm Thomas, and DJ Gay beating BYU at the 2010 Mountain West championship game in Las Vegas.

But that ranks a close second.

My all-time favorite Aztecs win was their 2014 upset of Kansas in Lawrence, where no one but KU *ever* wins.

And the best Aztecs' broadcast line?

During the 2020 basketball season, referring to the Aztecs' fifth-year senior Joshua Tomaic, who was from the Canary Islands, I said, "It's bizarre that there are no canaries found on the Canary Islands."

"Same with the Virgin Islands...No canaries there, either!"

Best Aztecs interview?

Many years ago, I did a halftime interview with former Aztecs linebacker Carl Weathers, who had come to fame in 1976 with his portrayal of Apollo Creed in *Rocky*, the first of the 83 or so Rocky movies.

I started to introduce him as "ex-Aztecs linebacker, now actor..."

Hearing that, he turned to me, eyes blazing, having, it appeared to me, a full-on Apollo flashback.

"What did you call me?"

Huh?

I started to reprise my introduction, but I truly didn't know what he was talking about.

That's when he interrupted me, saying, "Ted, there's no such thing as an ex-Aztec. Once an Aztec, always an Aztec. For *life*!"

Been a Carl Weathers fan ever since.

I've enjoyed working with Steve Fisher more than any coach, in any sport, at any level, at any station, in any city.

This is how much class Coach Fisher has: A few years ago, the Aztecs were about to play for the Mountain West championship in Vegas and the Fresno State women's team had just won the women's title.

Fresno State's locker room was located right next to the Aztecs' and their players were singing and shouting and laughing – they were so happy.

A security guard who was stationed in front of the women's locker room heard all that commotion and apparently had asked the team to keep the noise down.

Then, she knocked on the Aztecs' door and when Steve came to the door, she told him what she had done, that she had taken care of "the problem."

"What problem?"

"Well, they were making all kinds of noise and disturbing you guys," the guard said, "so I told them to cool it."

Coach Fisher then told the guard, who no doubt meant well, "Listen, do me a favor. Since you told them that, I'd like you to go back in there. And this time, I'd like you to apologize."

"Then, please tell them from me that they can whoop and holler and yell and jump up and down as much as they want – just like we're fixin' to do when we win the championship."

"Let them know that we have no problem with that whatsoever."

Now, tell me, what coach does that?

Coach Fisher, that's who.

In 2011, when Michigan was getting ready to pay Temple in the third round of the NCAA Tournament, a Temple fan by the name of Bill Cosby wrote a typewritten note to Steve Fisher, telling him how much he liked the Aztecs.

Obviously, he was going to root for Temple, but he made sure to tell Steve, "It's really going to be a great game. Tell your guys to keep up the great work."

Before the game, Steve read the letter to his team, then added one more sentence: "If you guys win this game," he said, "I'll invite you to come on the Cosby show in the near future."

Of course, Cosby didn't write that, but hey, coaches have to do whatever it takes to motivate their players.

After the game, which the Aztecs won, the players were in the locker room chanting, "Cosby, Cosby," thinking they were going to go on the show.

That's when Coach Fisher asked for their attention: "Eyes and ears here, please. That was a great win, guys. But I have an announcement to make. That Cosby show part? I made that up."

When we did booster banquets together, Steve would always tell the audience that, "When you mention San Diego State, people always mention Kawhi Leonard and defense."

And when I'd follow him as a speaker, I'd say, "I know Coach doesn't want to hear this, but wherever I go, when I mention San Diego State, they tell me they think of Kawhi Leonard, defense…and Coach Steve Fisher."

One of the greatest men I've ever known.

WE'LL BE RIGHT BACK AFTER THESE WORDS

Part 10

*"That's my mother and she hasn't
smiled or laughed for years."*

Everybody loves Ted Giannoulus' Famous Chicken. He started the whole sports mascot craze and nobody has ever done it better, then or since.

I truly believe that Ted and his Chicken suit deserve to be inducted into Baseball's Hall of Fame in Cooperstown for the impact he's had for starting the mascot craze, throughout the majors and the minors.

A few years ago, when I got together for lunch with Ted as part of a group of former Padres executives, he told this story:

After the crash of PSA Flight 182 in 1978, Ted was performing at a game when a young woman came up to him and said, pointing to a fan who was sitting a few rows away: "See that woman? You just made her smile and laugh."

Then she said, "Let me tell you, that's my mother and she hasn't smiled or laughed for a long time. My father, her husband, was the pilot of Flight 182. Not a smile, not a laugh since."

"But *you* made her smile and laugh. Thank you so much."

No, I didn't pay that guy to bring that sign. But I would've.
Whoever you are, I thank you.

41

The best of buddies

"You got Leitner's number? Let's call him."

DURING THE PANDEMIC, while the Padres were playing in the 2020 National League playoffs against the Dodger, I was sitting in our radio booth at Petco Park, getting ready to do play-by-play.

It was incredibly strange because at that moment, on the field below us, the Yankees were playing the Tampa Bay Rays in the American League playoffs.

On one of our TV monitors, along with the Padres game, we had the Yankees-Rays game on WTBS-TV's national telecast. To my surprise, I looked up and noticed that the camera was on me.

The graphic below was, "PADRE BROADCAST LEGEND, TED LEITNER."

As it turned out, a lot of my old buddies from my New York days, guys I hadn't seen or heard from in ages, saw that because, of course, they were watching the Yankees just like we used to do when we were growing up.

Almost from that moment on, I started to get a blizzard of calls, which I couldn't pick up because I was busy preparing for the broadcast. Believe me, they left *lots* of voicemails.

I'm sure it was a case of the guys calling each other and saying, "You got Leitner's number? You do? Let's call him."

After the Padres game, I played those voicemails and it was like I'd never left Yonkers. One guy who called, we had played football together at Roosevelt High and he was now a long-time high school coach in New York.

Typical of teammates, no matter how long it had been since we'd seen each other, he stuck the needle in, like nothing had changed in 50-plus years. It was like we were still the best of buddies and still teammates.

I turned on his voicemail and I heard, in this heavy "New Yaaawk" accent, "Hey, *Teddy Leitnah*, how in the world did *you* get to be such a legend?"

Another call was from the quarterback on that team and a couple of others, all in that heavy accent, and I thought, "Good God, did I talk like that?"

Whether I became a "legend" or not is debatable, but being on TV and radio has given me access to so many incredibly wonderful, famous, truly fascinating people.

Over the years, I've met astronauts – John Glenn and Wally Schirra, who rank as my all-time heroes – military leaders, presidents, ex-presidents, entertainers, millionaires and billionaires, and had so many experiences that I never could've dreamed of having.

The money was great, but believe me when I say that the people I've met through the years have been even better.

Like the time in 2001 when the touring company for the

Motown-themed musical, *Smokey Joe's Café*, came to town, starring one of my favorite soul performers, Gladys Knight, and her older brother, Bubba, famous as a Pip.

Earlier that day, a few hours before the show's opening performance, I had interviewed Bubba on my radio show.

Toward the end, he said, "We have a moment in the play where there's a song playing and we get somebody local, wherever we are across the country, who comes out and does a little cameo."

"You wanna do it?"

At first, I told him that I didn't want to do it because I knew I'd be a fish out of water. I told him I was a lousy actor, but Bubba insisted.

That night, I showed up an hour or so before showtime, and was greeted by Gladys, who's a terrific song stylist and very charming, just like Bubba.

After a member of the troupe handed me a green jester's hat, Gladys told me what they wanted me to do.

During their rendition of *Charlie Brown*, the Coasters' song from the '50s, I was supposed to rush on stage and say the classic lyric, "Why's everybody always pickin' on me?"

When my cue came, I went on stage, hit my mark, then said, referring to my love-hate relationship with viewers, "Why *IS* everybody always pickin' on me?"

The audience went nuts. They loved it.

Seconds later, I got the hell off the stage as fast as I could. And I thought to myself, "I really didn't want to do this, but I'm so glad I did."

It was so cool.

In the 1990s, another of my all-time favorites, the great Jerry

Lewis, lived aboard his yacht at the San Diego Marriott Marina to escape the Vegas heat during the summer.

This time, he happened to be in town with the road-show revival production of the Broadway musical, *Damn Yankees*, in a starring role as the Devil.

I had interviewed Jerry a few times on my talk show, and we had become friends. A few times, at our invitation, he joined Jerry Coleman and me in the booth, which was always a treat.

Based on our friendship, plus the fact that I'd always been a huge fan, going back to when I was growing up, he asked me if I'd like to introduce the play on opening night at San Diego's downtown Civic Theatre.

Of course, I said yes.

Contrary to his image, Jerry told me, "Don't make a big deal out of me. This is an ensemble piece."

I said, "Jerry, your name's above the title of the play. You're the *star*."

"I don't care," he said. "You can introduce me any way you'd like. But we're all in this together."

"OK, Jer, you got it."

That night, just before the curtain went up, I was waiting for my cue to go out.

The plan was that I'd walk out "cold" through a small opening in the middle of the curtain, without any introduction at all, talk for a few minutes about the play and my friendship with Jerry, then introduce the show.

Sounded easy enough.

Now I was backstage, about 15 minutes until showtime and I could hear the orchestra getting the audience all primed up with those terrific Leiber & Stoller songs.

My heart started beating like crazy, as if I really *was* a featured performer in this classic Broadway show, except that I wasn't.

I heard the stage manager on the PA backstage, say, "All right, everybody, two minutes. Let's have a great show."

I thought, "Uh, oh, I've made a big mistake. What am I doing here? Whatever you do, don't blow it."

Just in time, it occurred to me that I'd given speeches to thousands of groups at luncheons and banquets. And that I'd served as MC for so many events at Qualcomm and Petco in front of 40,000, even 60,000 people.

The problem was, in the back of my mind, I was still the kid who would cut class so I wouldn't have to give a speech in front of 15 or so fellow students. And this was no banquet, no ballgame. This was a big-time Broadway production.

When my stage call came, I walked out into the spotlight – with no introduction – and the crowd broke out into wild applause.

They knew who I was, and I then felt at home.

At that instant, I thought, "Wow, I guess you're *not* that little schmuck from Yonkers anymore."

It was so awesome. The audience laughed and applauded and the whole thing worked.

As I walked off the stage, I was elated – and relieved.

Another time when I had the honor of introducing Jerry Lewis was at Qualcomm when he sang the National Anthem before a Padres game.

Again, in contrast to his image, he said, "Don't mention the

Muscular Dystrophy telethon and don't make a big deal out of me."

In that situation, at least I was on my "home turf" and I felt great about being there.

By contrast, I felt way less than great when Roseanne Barr infamously sang the National Anthem before a Padres game in 1990.

She didn't sing the anthem so much as desecrate it.

Did I say *sing* the anthem? I meant screech like someone who got their hand slammed in a car door.

Trust me, you screech during the anthem and grab your crotch, you know all hell's gonna break out in a military town.

And it did.

Tom Werner, the Padres' general managing partner and a successful TV producer, had watched Roseanne's "performance" from his owner's box.

Knowing that media members would soon be racing up to his box to get his reaction, he locked the door and refused to come out.

Later, when I asked him about that, he said, "Hey, I'm right in the middle of negotiating a $50 million deal to syndicate *Roseanne*. You think I'm going to insult her by telling the media what I thought about her performance? Stupid, I am not."

After that game, I went back to the Channel 8 studio and got a call from Dick Freeman, who was then the Padres' CEO.

"Ted, will you do me a favor?"

"Sure, what's that?"

"Try not to beat the hell out of us tonight."

My response was, "Sorry, Dick, no can do."

42

A good ol' boy

"Hey, you hit it right on the head."

AROUND THE START OF SPRING TRAINING in late February of 1999, I had just arrived at the Padres' complex in Peoria after flying into Phoenix from doing an Aztecs basketball game on the road.

As I walked through the clubhouse, I saw a familiar face, someone I thought I recognized but wasn't quite sure. His head down, he was wearing a cowboy hat, and was intently autographing baseballs by the dozens.

At first, I walked past him, then turned around to take a second look. Sure enough, I knew who it was.

"254 East Bennett Hall," I said.

He looked up and said, "Oklahoma State, right?"

Hearing that exchange, he got up and brought over a chair from the next stall and invited me to sit down with him.

It was like we'd known each other for years, which is what anyone who's ever been lucky enough to meet Garth Brooks says about him, because it's true. He's a country superstar who's also a good ol' boy from Oklahoma.

He told me how he went to Oklahoma State in the early 1980s on a track scholarship as, of all things, a javelin thrower, which I never would've guessed.

We talked about the fraternity I was in, Phi Kappa Tau, and the one he was in, Alpha Gamma Rho, and then we talked about his first few years of trying to make it big.

He shared stories about my all-time favorite country performers like Willie Nelson, Waylon Jennings, and Merle Haggard, which happen to be his favorites, too.

To me, the thing about getting to know Garth Brooks was that he was happy to sign all those baseballs and more than happy to spend time talking to me, even though we'd just met.

He's devoted to his craft, devoted to his fans and never forgets where he came from.

To put it simply, he "gets it" – that fame and adulation means you have to give back to those who helped make you a success.

Later that spring, Garth invited Tim Flannery, the Padres' third-base coach at the time and a very talented musician, to come to the Wrigley Mansion in Phoenix for a country-music jam session.

That's where Garth was renting, so he invited Flan to jam and drink beer with him.

I said, "Flan! Flan! How come you didn't call me to come over?"

This was before cell phones, so all Tim could say was, "Hey, I didn't know where you were staying, so I didn't have your number," which was true.

Come on, Flan," I told him. "You and Garth Brooks? Singin', pickin', and jammin'? I would've loved that!"

Two of my favorite people.

One of my favorite Padres quotes comes from Flan.

When Dick Williams was the Padres' manager, Flan said, "When I retire, the first thing I want to do is buy a glass-bottom car so I can see the look on Dick's face when I run him over."

Get the picture?

As manager, Dick was a tough guy and I'm sure others felt the same way as Flan did. But they sure learned a lot about baseball and how to win.

When I was the MC for Dick's induction into the Padres' Hall of Fame, I gave him a big flourish of an introduction.

As he passed me on the way to the microphone, he leaned in and said, "It's about f---in' time you said something nice about me."

Being a California boy, Flan would take his wife Donna to the beach to enjoy the sunset wherever they happened to be in Southern California.

On a Padres' road trip back East, I'm told, Flan decided to drive down to the Jersey Shore to catch the sunset, complete with a bottle of wine, baguette and cheese.

He and Donna waited and waited until they realized that the sun doesn't set on the East Coast like it does on the West Coast.

I realize that Flan hates it when I tell that story and even denies that it happened. But I got it from a really good source. So, sorry, Flan.

It's kind of like when the Braves' John Smoltz was leaving a hotel room and noticed that his shirt was a bit wrinkled. The iron was still hot, so he decided to do a little touch-up – while he was wearing the shirt.

He slightly burned his chest, but the story, which he denies, took on a life of its own.

Once again, that's what baseball teammates are for, to rat you out, throw you under the bus, and get a good laugh at your expense.

Unfortunately, Flan's friend, Garth Brooks, didn't have much success as a player that spring.

Used sparingly as a pinch-hitter and outfielder, he mustered only one hit in 22 at-bats, including a walk when the umpire called a ball on a pitch that was right down the middle.

Yet, before and after games, I'd see him signing autographs for what seemed like hours along the fence, with fans clamoring for him to sign whatever they handed to him.

He didn't disappoint anybody and for that alone, he's one of the most remarkable superstars I've ever known.

The stories about Garth's kindness and generosity are true, like the one where one of his female fans held up a handwritten sign saying she was pregnant, when he stopped the show and walked over to her.

He said, "Hey, congratulations and I'll tell you what. If I'm still alive when that boy or girl goes to college, I'll pay for it."

True story, and there have been many others, where a young female fan would have a sign saying how much she loved him and others saying they were going through chemo treatments, and he would give them his guitar during the show.

He's that kind of person, and it's not an act because I saw

it up-close. I saw it before games, after games, and in the clubhouse.

The story of Garth Brooks is a great American business/ showbiz story. Maybe that's part of why he "gets" it, but to me, it's also because he's an Oklahoman.

I spent a decade living in Oklahoma and believe me, they're the friendliest, nicest people you'd ever want to meet. We may have huge political differences, but you can't have better friends and better neighbors than Oklahomans.

Steve Garvey "got it" when he was with the Padres in the 1980s. As far as I could tell, he never turned down an autograph request.

Some of his teammates with the Dodgers and then the Padres thought he was something of a phony, but I never thought so.

He was a guy who, like Garth, was beholden to his fans and realized early on that his success didn't happen in a vacuum.

There were a few "other" requests for his time and attention that perhaps he should've declined. Who could forget those bumper stickers, "Steve Garvey is NOT my Padre"?

I was among several speakers at an offseason banquet, sharing the dais with Steve and the late Tommy Lasorda.

As I put it: "The thing with The Garv is that he remembers being a little kid at Vero Beach" – where the Dodgers trained for many years – "and hanging out with his dad, Joe, who was the team's bus driver, with the players tousling his hair and telling him to stay in school and be good and all that stuff."

I went on: "Whenever he's asked for his autograph, he

makes every effort to comply, especially if it's a youngster who asks him."

After the banquet, Lasorda came up to me and said, "Hey, you hit it right on the head."

Then he told me this story, which I've cleaned up as best I could.

Tommy said: "I tried to do that, too, because I was a minor leaguer for 1,000 years, and I got turned down for an autograph by some major-leaguer when I went to a game in Philadelphia. It pissed me off so much."

Years later, Tommy was pitching against this guy in Montreal.

The first pitch Tommy threw was right at the guy's head, and sent him sprawling on the dirt. The guy started to take a few steps toward the mound and Tommy said, "C'mon, I'll kick your ass."

After the game, one of the sportswriters asked him, "What was it with you and that guy? Why'd you throw at him?"

This was Tommy's response: "Because he blew me off when I asked him for an autograph. He never broke stride, just looked at me like I wasn't even there, and I never forgot that."

That was Tommy.

His players loved to push the right buttons to get him ranting and raving, and it didn't take much.

My friend Jerry Reuss, who pitched for the Dodgers in the 1980s, told me the story about when Tommy was a pitchman for a popular diet product.

Hoping to jerk him around, a group of players would sneak into the closet in Tommy's office, take his spare uniform and send it to a seamstress to take it in.

Then, Tommy, having lost a few pounds, would put on that uniform and just blow a gasket because it wouldn't fit.

"How the hell could this happen?" he'd yell. "Here I'm starving myself all week, and I haven't lost a damn pound!"

Just outside Tommy's office, Reuss and his teammates were busting a gut.

<hr>

Being as beloved as Tommy was, when the Dodgers were on the road, he made sure that he never had to pay for a meal.

In whatever city the Dodgers were, he'd bring a bunch of his players and coaches for a post-game meal at his favorite Italian restaurant. There, they'd wait for his signal.

If they got it, that was the sign that he had sweet-talked the owner into picking up the check.

So, it was, "Knock yourselves out, boys."

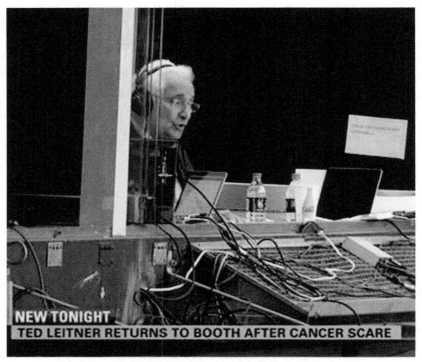

NEW TONIGHT
TED LEITNER RETURNS TO BOOTH AFTER CANCER SCARE

A screen shot of Channel's 8 feature story after I returned to the radio booth after my cancer scare.

Not many standing ovations in my career. Thank you, Padres fans.

43

That slapped me in the face

"The Big Friar in the Sky was still looking out for me."

I'VE HAD A FEW LIFE-CHANGING MOMENTS in my time, for better and worse, but what happened in April 2017 not only changed my life, it probably saved my life.

I thought I had cancer, when a mass showed up on my kidney on an ultrasound following a CAT scan on my liver.

All I heard was that one word, "mass," and unless you're Catholic, that's the last thing you want to hear.

Right away, my urologist confirmed the diagnosis.

"I've got to tell you, it's a tumor, a big one, the size of a golf ball," he told me. "And I'll be honest with you, I've never seen one that big that *wasn't* cancer."

Well, there goes *that* day.

The next day, I met with another urologist, who told me, "We have to operate. The tumor is right in the middle, so we can't just use the robotic surgery to remove just the tumor and leave a partial working kidney.

"We have to remove the entire kidney."

They did another CAT scan to see if the mass had spread outside the kidney.

Right after that test, I rejoined the Padres in San Francisco, and took the doctor's call while I was in a cab going to the ballpark.

What a sweet moment, when your doctor says, "It hasn't spread."

Simply lovely.

Because if the tumor does leave the kidney, then chemo is not an option and you're in a heap of trouble.

At that moment, I got the feeling that the Big Friar in the Sky was still looking out for me.

Looking back, I made a mistake when I announced on Twitter that I was taking a leave of absence from the Padres because, as I phrased it, "I've been diagnosed with cancer."

What I should've said was that my doctors were 98% sure it was cancer.

A few days later, I went into surgery and they removed the bad kidney. When I was recovering in post-op, I got the word that it was benign.

All three doctors with whom I had discussed my case were astounded – happy for me, but astounded.

My primary care doctor, Dr. Ryan Dominguez, called me and said, "I would've bet my mortgage that it was cancer."

I repeat: The Big Friar in the Sky was looking out for Uncle Teddy.

The next morning, still in recovery at Sharp Hospital, I was pushing my walker very slowly down the hall. This older fellow opened his door, saw me coming and said, "Ted Leitner! I listen to you all the time!"

"Thanks," I said, "how're *you* doing?"

He said, "How am I doing? I woke up this morning! It's

a great day! Nothing's bothering me! I'm on this side of the grass!"

Hearing that was like a slap in the face, as in, "Listen to what he's trying to tell you. He woke up this morning and he's so happy just to be alive."

You should be, too.

I've never been that way. I've always been accused of being a complainer and a whiner.

One time, I was standing in line at the KFMB cafeteria and Larry Himmel was in front of me.

I'm telling Larry that we've got to do this and we've got to do that, on and on.

Larry slowly turned around and said, "Ted, you know that huge telescope at Palomar?"

"No."

"They've theorized that if you took that telescope with all of its power and combined it with the even bigger one on the Big Island of Hawaii, with all of that combined power to look into the heavens, they still couldn't find anything that you should be bitching about."

Even when great success came my way, as it has, I'd feel like I had to complain about something or another.

Not about the jobs I had, but I'd complain because I was doing too much, even though I loved the work.

It's like the old Tommy Lasorda line, that half the people don't want to hear your problems, and the other half are glad you got them.

I also like the Cameron Diaz line that I saw a few years ago in *Parade* magazine: "If you don't appreciate what you have, you'll never be happy."

Now you tell me?

I realize that I was considered a pain in the ass by a lot of people I worked with. I'm convinced of it, and I've talked to a lot of them in the interim, apologized and thanked them for all they did for me.

———— ❧ ————

Now, luckily, I've still got one kidney left and it's functioning just fine.

There's a cyst in the remaining kidney that they found in a follow-up CAT scan, but they keep telling me not to worry about it.

Yeah, right.

Telling me not to worry is like telling me not to talk, but my eyesight is also a problem. Three diseases in the right eye, glaucoma in both.

Hope I'm not complaining too much again, because I'm lucky to have the No. 1-rated glaucoma surgeon and researcher in the world, Dr. Robert Weinreb, who's director of the Shiley Eye Institute in La Jolla, among many more credits.

I see him every four months, and so far, so good.

Dr. Weinreb operated on my bad eye, and I'm convinced that he prolonged my career by doing so.

When I say that he's No. 1 in the world, I mean it. When Willie Mays had his glaucoma problem, who did he go to? Dr. Weinreb.

Same thing with Kirby Puckett, who had vision problems when he was with the Twins. Same with my friend, the late, great Duke Snider.

I'm forever in Dr. Weinreb's debt.

44

The last line of defense

"Why don't you just back off?"

THANK GOD, I HAVEN'T HAD MANY INCIDENTS where I said something on the air I shouldn't have, because those "mistakes" can be career-enders in this business, especially these days.

When San Diego State played New Mexico in the 2014 Mountain West championship game in Las Vegas, I lost my mind.

I had just flown into Vegas after doing a Padres spring training game, so I had my carry-on bag with me. I was going to leave right after the game to fly back to Phoenix and drive to Peoria for the next day's game.

I put my carry-on right next to me on the floor.

You must understand something about the security guards at Thomas and Mack Arena – all the visiting broadcasters talk about it. These guys act like they're guarding an Army base.

They think they're the last line of defense in protecting truth, justice and the American Way. Getting past their security checkpoints has always been nothing but a pain in the ass.

This time, it got to be halftime and I was walking past press row to get to the media room. I was with Darin Wong, who was then a member of the Aztecs' PR staff, and now handles Harvard's sports information.

As we were walking along the sideline, this big fellow, the supervisor who's always the most obnoxious guard in the building, looked at Darin, who was wearing a suit and tie, and saw that his media credential was partially obscured by his tie.

The guard barked at him, "Where's your credential?"

Darin then moved his tie so that his credential was more visible.

But before we could go on our way, this jerk said to Darin, "Wear that credential everywhere you go in this building."

I just lost it, and said to the guard, "Hey, as visiting media, we're supposed to be your guests. Who the hell do you think you're talking to? This is just a Mountain West basketball game. Do you really think we'd try to sneak in?"

"Why don't you just back off?"

No offense to the Mountain West, but this wasn't exactly the Final Four.

The guard glared at me and I glared back at him, and then Darin and I went to the media room.

During the last two minutes of the championship game, which was extremely close, that dipstick no doubt decided to dispatch one of his fellow dipsticks to grab my shoulder – during the broadcast! – and bust my stones.

He demanded that I move my carry-on because he claimed it was blocking the aisle, which it wasn't.

"*You have to move this suitcase*," he said, serious as he could be.

Nobody was walking up the steps or coming down the steps. My carry-on wasn't in anybody's way.

With less than a minute left in the game, this guy had interrupted my play-by-play, forcing me to turn around to see who the hell he was, which made me miss a New Mexico player going in for a fast-break layup that turned out to be the game-winning basket.

I just lost it.

Pissed out of my mind, I said to him, which went over the air: "What is your *problem*? Don't you know that I'm on the air here? You guys are the *worst* security guards in all of sports! What's the problem, if I don't move my suitcase, the terrorists win?"

Trying to regroup, I said to my listeners, "I apologize, but these security guards at Thomas and Mack Arena are just stupid. It's unbelievable, but these morons think the terrorists are here at the Mountain West tournament in Las Vegas!"

My on-air rant was picked up by Deadspin and went viral, which was more than slightly embarrassing.

That was the first time – and the last – I've ever completely lost it during a broadcast.

I had another case of, as we say in Latin, *broadcastus interruptus*, when my twins, Nick and Ryan, were small, maybe 5 or 6.

On Hudson & Bauer, I used to refer to them as Damian I and Damian II, from the movie *The Omen* – and one time I took them with me on a Padres road trip.

We happened to be in Milwaukee, in old County Stadium, and the twins were sitting in the loge section, just to the left of our booth.

I had bought them both small cups filled with Dippin' Dots, the ice cream with those little flavored dots that they've advertised for the past 20 years as the "ice cream of the future."

Hey, give it up, they ain't!

Using their plastic spoons, they were flipping dots into the air, and they were landing on the backs of a few fans' heads and necks.

One of the fans called for an usher, who asked the kids who they were supposed to be with. After one of them pointed to the press box, the usher tracked down a deputy sheriff, standing guard at the press box entrance.

I was on the air, doing the game, when I got — oh, no, not *another* tap on the shoulder like in Las Vegas!

What the hell's going on?

But in contrast to that, this guy was smart enough or considerate enough to wait until we had a commercial break.

"I'm sorry to interrupt you, sir, but are those your kids out there?" he asked me, pointing to where the twins were sitting.

God help me, I had a flash thought to say, "Nope," but instead I said, "Yeah, what're they doing now?"

"Well, they're flipping their ice cream dots on the necks of the fans below."

I *thought* about telling the cop they weren't my kids because I remembered when my oldest son, Mark, had just started 7th grade of middle school.

It was the first day of classes and the teacher called his name during roll.

At recess, a couple of his new classmates came up to him and said, "Your name's Leitner, right?"

"Yeah."

"Is Ted Leitner your dad?"

"No."

After he had denied my very existence, he told me the story when he got home that night.

"I didn't know whether they were going to beat me up or what," he said. "I just panicked."

Oh, my God, is *that* what it's like to be my son?

I've been told by some people that, because I ad-libbed my Channel 8 sportscasts, it must've been easy for me.

A magazine writer once wrote about me, "He never prepares, he just always ad-libs."

Oh, no.

Not at all.

If I didn't spend nearly all my waking hours preparing for whatever I was going to do next, there's no way I could've done what I did for so long.

Because when you ad-lib, you've got to know something about what you're talking about.

And with all that I did during the 1980s and '90s — play-by-play for the Padres, the Chargers, and Aztecs' football and basketball, plus my daily KFMB talk show, doing the 5, 6 and 11 o'clock sports on Channel 8 five days a week, and cutting commercials and talking to groups, which I did a lot.

Even though most of it was ad-libbed, I had to prepare for each one.

I'd be at home reading a stack of newspapers and magazines, studying like crazy, and my kids would say, "Hey, Dad, let's do something."

But I'd have to say I couldn't because I was getting ready to do whatever was coming up next.

Mere seconds after wrapping up a Padres game, no matter

what time it was, I'd be thinking, "OK, what're you going to do tomorrow on H&B?"

And, "What are you going to do for your Channel 8 segment?"

And so on.

This was all before the Internet and smart phone days, so it really did detract from time I should've been spending with my family.

But I didn't see my life that way.

I regret it now, believe me.

45

All the sights and sounds

"I can't see a thing!"

GOING INTO THE 2020 SEASON, I had made the decision that it was going to be my final season of doing Padres' play-by-play. I'd consulted with the Padres, and was OK with that decision.

Then the pandemic shut everything down.

That 60-game regular season was bizarre in just about every way possible – except for the games. And I'm so grateful that I had the opportunity to do them.

I didn't miss the travel because, God knows, I've done enough of that to last a lifetime. But I sure missed the game atmosphere – the fans, the cheering, all the sights and sounds of being at the ballpark, especially Petco.

Having to do road games from our booth at Petco, now *that* was a challenge.

Our first few games reminded me of when I was growing up, when I'd pretend that I was doing play-by-play for whatever sport I was watching, baseball or football or basketball, didn't matter.

Though I had no discernable early signs of talent, I'd turn

down the volume and pretend I was Mel Allen or Lindsey Nelson or Marty Glickman and do the games for an audience of one: me.

The only other time I had done that was when Tim Flannery auditioned for the Padres radio broadcasts back in the early 2000s at Qualcomm Stadium.

We were watching video of a previous game, so the executives could decide if Flannery and I worked well together.

C'mon, who doesn't get along with Flan?

Initially, the setup drove me nuts because I couldn't talk about the basics, like setting the defensive alignment or getting an accurate read on the types of pitches, judging the height and distance of fly balls, that sort of thing.

At one point during our "broadcast," I turned to Flan and said, "This is absolute BS. I can't see a thing!"

I had great trepidation about doing those 2020 games, even though I knew it would only be a shortened regular season, plus the playoffs that happily followed.

Speaking for my radio partner Jesse Agler, as well as for our TV team, Don and Mud, we were grateful to have *any* games.

I've got to credit MLB because they provided us and all the other teams' broadcasters, with an additional four-quadrant screen that gave us four different "live" video angles.

Thanks to that screen, Jesse and I were able to see more clearly what was happening than we could by just peering at a single main screen.

That came in handy in describing things like infield shifts and trying to calculate the distance of deep fly balls, when we couldn't tell if the ball had been caught or was a ground-rule double or a home run.

That added screen prevented us from sounding like we didn't know what we were talking about.

In 2021, my friend John Sterling, who's a terrific play-by-play guy for the Yankees, got caught by watching a replay that he thought was live action.

What he saw was a video replay of a home run by the guy who was coming up for his second at-bat. John mistakenly called the videoed home run as if it was happening at that moment, and got ripped by the New York tabloids and social media.

Hey, if it can happen to John Sterling, it could've happened to me and Jesse.

But it didn't.

I would frequently repeat the silent prayer that was verbalized by astronaut Alan Shepard, when he was sitting on top of the first American launch into space.

Speaking out-loud to the private NASA sound feed, he said, "Please, God, don't let me screw up."

After a while, I'm convinced that we became good at describing what was going on, even if we weren't at the actual road games.

As we often said to each other, "We can only say what we can see."

During those broadcasts, I wasn't lamenting that 2020 would be my last season. I was just happy that the players and owners reached a labor agreement in enough time to *have* a season.

To make matters much better, the Padres went out in their spiffy new brown-and-gold unis and had one of their best seasons in a long time.

After that NL Division playoff series win over St. Louis, it was so wonderful to see the fans celebrate that night in the Gaslamp Quarter, honking horns and, as Jack Buck once famously said, "Go crazy, folks, go crazy!"

As I walked to my car, I could hardly get to the parking structure as hundreds of ecstatic fans came up to me.

Fans honking their horns as they went by, waving Padres banners out the windows, screaming and yelling, "Go Padres!" – it was a remarkable moment.

I thought, man, this is so cool.

That's the power my Padres have to bring an entire community together.

And in this case, in the midst of a pandemic.

It was sweet to be part of all that, plus the fact that the Padres had beaten the Cardinals made it so much sweeter, after losing to them in past playoffs.

I was grateful to share in that moment of euphoria, a feeling that doesn't happen very often in sports, especially given the Padres' history of coming close a few times, but never winning the whole thing.

That feeling may not last forever, but there's nothing like it.

When the 2020 season was finally over, after the Dodgers beat the Padres to win the National League championship, I didn't want to make that moment about me, so I didn't announce that I'd just finished my last Padres broadcast.

For me to be in the midst of those wildly happy, delirious Padres fans, who were saying all these wonderful, complimentary things to me, that was just as good as being able to say goodbye at the end of my final game.

Even though I didn't say it, I knew it was time to say goodbye.

46

Just me being me

"I've always wanted to ask you this question."

IT COULD BE A FACTOR OF GETTING OLDER, but these past few years I've made an effort to apologize to as many people as possible.

So, for anything I might've done or said that I shouldn't have, or anything else that might've hurt someone's feelings, including people I used to work with, I'm sorry, I really am.

That brings me to the time the late, great Charlie Jones, the longtime La Jolla-based NBC sportscaster who was a good friend, introduced me at a banquet where he was the MC.

I was sitting with my then-wife and Charlie proceeded to introduce everyone on the dais.

He said, "This is Ted's wife."

"Why don't you stand up? You know, I've always wanted to ask you this question: How the hell do you put up with him?"

Ouch.

The audience thought it was hilarious, but she just smiled and the moment passed.

But I don't want to let *this* moment pass without saying, "Thank you, thank you from the bottom of my heart for putting up with me all these years."

———— ✕✕✕ ————

For those of you who, unlike Larry Lucchino, never acquired a taste for anchovies – or in this case, me – I apologize for any aggravation I may have caused you.

If you yelled like crazy at your radio or TV when I said things you didn't agree with, I apologize. That was just me being me.

Even if you didn't care for what I did, I truly thank you for watching and listening all these years.

Because for me, it's been wonderful.

OVERTIME

Owners I have known

"I'd better keep him as a friend."

IN MY BUSINESS, IF YOU THINK you're so brave and outrageous and you love to stir things up, as I did, there's no way you're keeping your job unless your bosses support you.

The Padres' owners, each in their own way, protected my ass from getting fired.

Now, ladies and gentlemen, a few words about some of the owners and executives I've aggravated through the years.

Ray Kroc

When I first got to know him, I had to pinch myself that I even *knew* Ray Kroc.

I mean, he was the founder of McDonald's, the man who changed the way we eat in this country and, in some respects, throughout the world. Think of it: Before Ray Kroc came along, there was no such thing as fast food.

It was Ray Kroc, tenacious bulldog that he was, who made McDonald's what it became.

When Ray had his office at Qualcomm, I happened to be walking by and he asked me to come in. He was in a wheelchair then because he had suffered a stroke. We were talking about baseball and McDonald's and business, having a great time and I couldn't believe it.

Here I was, a guy who didn't know anything about business, and I'm getting the chance to pick the brain of one of the most amazing and creative businessmen in history.

At one point, he said, "You know how you compete, don't you, Ted? If your competitor is drowning, you stick a hose in his mouth."

I thought to myself, "Wow, this old guy is one very tough businessman. I'd better keep him as a friend, because I'd never want him for an enemy."

Through his son-in-law, Padres president Ballard Smith, I knew that, for some misguided reason, Ray believed everything I said on Channel 8 about the Padres.

And Ballard would always tell him, "Don't watch that guy. He doesn't know a damn thing."

Then Ballard would come to me and say, "Hey, Ray thinks you know what you're talking about when you give suggestions on what we should do. And then he tells me to do it."

"Do me favor: Cut it out!"

When the Padres were talking to Reggie Jackson after he left the Oakland A's to become a free agent, Reggie came down to San Diego for a face-to-face interview with Ray.

Ray later told me that Reggie asked for a huge salary and an outrageous signing bonus. Plus, as part of the deal, he wanted a full-length fur coat for himself.

That was *not* how you negotiated with Ray Kroc. He wasn't

used to getting those kinds of demands from his McDonald's employees.

Ray's comment to me was, "This guy, Reggie Jackson, he thinks he's God. But he's not... I am."

In January 1974, when the Padres had all but packed up and moved to Washington D.C., Ray inquired about buying the franchise.

The asking price was $12 million, which wasn't a problem for Ray, who had made $200 million the day McDonald's went public. He was determined to buy a major-league team after he'd just been turned down in his bid to buy the Chicago Cubs.

Years later, Joan Kroc told me the story about how Ray had his financial rep place a call to the Padres and the conversation went something like this:

"How will Mr. Kroc and his group be paying?"

"There is no 'group' – Mr. Kroc *is* the group."

"Well, how will Mr. Kroc be paying?"

"He will write you a check."

And that's what he did.

Joan Kroc

After Ray died in early 1984, his widow, Joan, took over running the team.

Before that, I didn't know Joan very well, but later on, we became very close friends. She was wonderful.

When my twins were about to be born, she asked me if she could be their godmother, and of course, I said yes. My mother didn't raise any fools.

Joan showed up at the hospital to congratulate us. Then she

called her attorney and directed her to set aside $50,000 each as trust funds for the twins.

Thanks to Joan's generosity, my kids were in great shape. Me, not so much.

Joan loved the late Father Joe Carroll, who was among San Diego's leading advocates for the homeless and those in need.

And Father Joe loved Joan.

When he was seeking a large donation to make Father Joe's Villages become a reality a few blocks from Petco Park, Joan's contribution totaled almost $3 million.

Generous? Oh, yeah.

That's why they called her "Saint Joan of Arches."

Before she passed away much too soon in 2003 at age 75, she had donated nearly $3 billion to charitable causes she believed in, including the arts, education, health care, AIDS and cancer research, and world peace.

One time, lucky me, I was invited to join Joan and a select group of her friends for a weekend aboard her very large and very luxurious $40 million yacht.

After a Padres game in Atlanta, leading into the All-Star break, Joan arranged for me and my wife to fly to Bermuda on her private jet, a Gulfstream IV, to meet her at the docks.

The next day, as the yacht's crew was preparing our brunch, Joan, in a mock hoity-toity voice, called out to another sizable yacht that was berthed next to hers, "Excuse me, sir, do you have any Grey Poupon?"

That was so Joan.

The fellow was fresh out of Grey Poupon. But somehow, we managed.

———∞∞∞———

Of course, Joan knew almost nothing about baseball, which she didn't mind admitting.

When Ray was about to buy the Padres, he told her he was thinking about buying "the San Diego Padres."

Much later, Joan told me, "I swear to you, I truly thought he was telling me that he wanted to buy a religious group, like a monastery. When I asked Ray if that's what he meant, he laughed and said, 'No, it's a *baseball* team.'"

That was Joan, generous and caring and not above laughing at herself.

And I loved her for it.

Tom Werner

Understand this about Tom Werner: He loves baseball, he loved the Padres, he loved San Diego, and he bought the franchise at the very worst time.

This was the time of collusion when MLB owners were forced to pay over $280 million to the players after being caught colluding against free-agent signings.

This was also about the time when CBS paid $1.1 billion to Major League Baseball for a four-year contract, then the largest TV sports deal in history.

All of a sudden, an awful lot of money was getting thrown around and Tom's ownership group – the so-called "Gang of 15" of local minority owners – was in no mood to spend that kind of money.

When he was in high school, Tom was so obsessed with sports and TV that his career guidance counselor told him, "Look, you can't just think about sports and television all your life. If you do, you'll never amount to anything."

That young man became a Harvard graduate and a multi-millionaire.

So much for *that* career advice.

When Tom's production firm, Carsey-Werner, first pitched the Cosby show, each of the major networks said, "Nah, too boring."

One of the early episodes was based on the little girl's goldfish dying, and then the Cosby family consoled her. The network exec said, "That's it? No arguments? No car chases? No arrests?"

All the networks turned it down and Tom had to put his home up for collateral to shoot the pilot and the first six episodes. Then NBC decided to take a chance.

That led to *The Cosby Show* being the No. 1-rated show for five straight years, and NBC becoming the No. 1 TV network.

Tom told me that he thought his life was going to end when he was approached by reliever Randy Myers in the Padres' clubhouse.

Myers, you may remember, was like one of those survivalists with his Army fatiques and *Soldier of Fortune* magazines and hunting knives in his locker.

One time, when Tom went to the Padres' clubhouse to

mingle with the players, Myers immediately got in his face, saying, "How dare you allow this Ice T guy to have that 'Cop Killer' song on your label!"

"He's nothing but a disgrace, and that song is a disgrace to our country!"

Meanwhile, Tom is wondering, what the hell is this guy talking about?

Turns out, Myers didn't realize he was talking to Tom Werner, *not* the namesake owner of the Time-Warner record label.

As Gilda Radner's Emily Litella used to say on *Saturday Night Live*, "Never mind!"

One day, at a time when Padres' fans were outraged by the so-called "Fire Sale" of 1992, Tom invited me to his place on the beach at Del Mar.

As the two of us headed out for a swim, we noticed this group of guys, maybe 50 feet away, staring at us.

I told Tom, "They're staring at you," and he said, "No, they're staring at *you*."

That's when one of them shouted, "God Almighty, where's a tsunami when you need one?"

When Tom sold his majority ownership of the Padres in 1994, he was more than happy to move on. And most Padres fans said, good riddance.

But his results – three World Series titles – as a part-owner of the Boston Red Sox, along with partner John Henry deserves respect.

Plenty of Padres fans with long memories will strongly disagree, I'm sure.

John Moores

Everyone should be lucky enough to work for someone like John Moores in their profession as I did in mine.

When people talk about a business being run "like a family," usually it's not. But when John was in charge, he ran the Padres like a family.

On road trips where wives and girlfriends were invited, the Moores family would make sure that all their rooms had gift baskets when they checked in.

Virtually anything his players, coaches, and front office needed to do their jobs better or more effectively, was theirs for the asking.

His constant question was, "What do you need?"

John asked that very question of then-Aztecs AD Rick Bay at a charity event. The answer to that is now standing on 55th Street with the Sports Deck, Tony Gwynn Stadium, and other on-campus buildings. All to the tune of $50 million.

Like all the other owners, I'm sure there were times when John saw me on Channel 8 and scratched his head, wondering how I could be so critical of the team while I was also doing the Padres' radio play-by-play with Jerry.

I was told that Larry Lucchino, John's president/CEO and *the* guiding force for Petco Park – and what a dynamic team they were – once placed a whiteboard inside the Padres' office entrance.

On the board was written, TED LEITNER, and two words on either side, YES or NO.

During that week, team employees were supposed to cast their vote, like in the Roman Coliseum, thumbs up or thumbs down.

I don't know if they were trying to get rid of me, or just trying to get a pulse on who I was and what I was.

That gave me pause, because, as John has often kidded me since, he agrees with Larry's classic line that I'm an acquired taste.

With John and Larry running the show, along with Charles Steinberg in charge of the team's brilliant promotions and public relations, what a front office that was, as good as MLB has ever seen.

Peter Seidler

Let me put this directly and sincerely: All the Padres' broadcasters have loved Peter Seidler since Day 1 of his ownership.

He's low-key, soft-spoken, down-to-earth and he loves baseball – just like John Moores.

I don't know how much Peter has been affected by being at death's door with his own cancer scares, which were much more serious than mine. But there's never been an owner in San Diego sports history like him.

Think of it: No one in baseball had the slightest idea that the Padres had any chance of signing Manny Machado – no one but Peter. Everyone just assumed that Manny would sign with the White Sox or the Phillies.

But Peter put together what was then the biggest contract in MLB history, $300 million for 10 years, and Manny became a Padre. And Manny is the happiest he's ever been.

This was after Peter had agreed to big contracts with Eric

Hosmer, Wil Myers, and then Peter topped himself with that 14-year, $340 million deal with the simply amazing Fernando Tatis Jr.

I know this: Padres fans believe in Peter Seidler, they trust him, they admire him, and they know his heart will always be in the right place.

I've never seen that level of fan devotion and loyalty to any other ownership here in any sport.

They know he truly wants to win – and win now.

Photo Album

The cover of "Leitner Strikes," published in 1985. You know what? I've never read it. I already know what I said.

Tiana Seau Jr. Love you, man.

Hey, the money was good, but this was even better. My reserved parking space at Qualcomm Stadium, as created by a group of Aztecs football fans.

Thank you, guys and girls.

My dear mother holding me during the summer when I was 2. Notice how I'm holding her thumb in my right hand and not letting go?

At a family gathering with my two older brothers, me (at left),
Mike (center) and Lew.

No, Mom didn't put my name on ALL of my shirts, just this
one.

A Jerry Coleman-autographed baseball on display in the Hall of Heroes at Yankee Stadium. My guy Jer was big-time, but never acted like he thought he was.

The auditorium at Roosevelt High School, where I gave my first speech in front of a large crowd.

A few days before, there had been a fight in the stands during our football game. The school's leaders had me and the other co-captains tell our fellow students to "play nice."

During a master of ceremonies performance at Petco Park. A true privilege.

Apologies for the crease, but that's me, No. 40, from my high school yearbook.

Looks like I'm about to recover a fumble, which I did.

My mom and me on the beach one fine summer day long ago. Life was as good as it could ever be.

A screen shot taken from my interviews for the MLB Network special on Anthony Keith Gwynn.

VOICES

*A collection of quotes, anecdotes and reflections
from those who know Ted well.*

Compiled by John Freeman

SCOTT KAPLAN

OUTSPOKEN AND OUTRAGEOUS, with a biting sense of humor, Scott Kaplan has been a sports media force in San Diego for nearly 20 years.

He gets full credit for the moniker of "Uncle Teddy," which, as he explains below, he dubbed Ted Leitner when Kaplan first came to San Diego in 2003.

"If Jerry Coleman was San Diego's grandfather, then Ted Leitner is everybody's Uncle Teddy."

He previously hosted long-running shows on XTRA-AM and The Mighty 1090-AM, paired with former Chargers linebacker Billy Ray Smith.

Since 2020, Kaplan has hosted "Kaplan & Crew" weekdays on The Mightier 1090-AM, along with the show's expansive social-media network.

When I first came to San Diego, people would say to me, "My God, you're like the next young Ted Leitner."

At that time, I was 30 years old and I didn't really understand the reference. One day, I was at the Chargers' training camp and Ted was there because he was still calling their games on radio.

I walked up to him and said, "Hi, Ted, my name is Scott Kaplan and I'm a new radio personality in town."

"I've been told that you're the guy who laid the groundwork for a younger, obnoxious, Jewish, East Coast guy like me to

make his way in a town that doesn't have too many personalities like that – except for you."

I told him it was an honor to meet him and, starting with that first meeting, we soon became very close friends, both professionally and personally, which I'm very proud of.

As I got to know him better, on- and off-air, I came to realize the love and admiration I had for him, and that he was truly a trailblazer in our business, someone who had a lot of opinions, not just about sports, but about a wide variety of subjects and was, let's face it, impossible to ignore.

At some point, it struck me that Ted reminded me, very much, of my own Uncle Sheldon when I was growing up. Uncle Sheldon was loud and boisterous and funny, and wherever he went, he was the life of the party.

So, I just started referring to Ted as "Uncle Teddy" because I felt like his favorite nephew, which I still do. Everywhere I went, that's how I referred to Ted, even when we were talking to each other.

The great thing is, he enjoyed it and, of course, he was so famous and so recognizable as a personality, that me calling him Uncle Teddy really caught on.

Now, it's been almost 20 years and the name has stuck to the point where he's become all of San Diego's uncle. If Jerry Coleman was San Diego's grandfather, then Ted Leitner is everybody's Uncle Teddy.

We all know that Ted could've made a lot more money and had more fame if he'd gone somewhere else. But like so many of us, he fell in love with San Diego and he became a legend. There's never been anyone like him and never will be.

We love our Uncle Teddy.

JESSE AGLER

A MEMBER OF THE PADRES' BROAD-CAST TEAM since 2014, Jesse Agler became the team's lead play-by-play radio voice in 2021.

Prior to that, he partnered with Ted Leitner on the Padres' flagship station 97.3 The Fan for the previous five seasons.

"He's never lost that mindset of being a 10-year-old kid at Yankee Stadium."

Before joining the Padres, Agler had been with the Miami Marlins as an on-air host, along with roles covering the NHL's Florida Panthers and the University of Miami's football and basketball radio broadcasts.

More than anything else, what comes to my mind when I think about Ted Leitner is that he's always been a relentless ball of energy.

When we started working together on a regular basis, it amazed me that his passion for baseball and for doing the broadcasts was still burning as hot as anyone I'd ever known.

What was equally amazing was that he never got cynical about doing the work that needs to be done, every day, every game, no matter how the team was doing on the field.

Believe me, there are an awful lot of people in this business who reach a certain cynicism fairly quickly. But with Ted, that never happened, even after some 40 years.

He's somehow kept his boyish joy and enthusiasm about the game. And as far as I can tell, he's never lost that mindset of being a 10-year-old kid at Yankee Stadium.

It didn't matter if it was Opening Day or it was late in the season and we were out of contention, he always seemed to bring the same energy to his broadcasts.

The thing about Ted is, he's a born entertainer and I'm sure he would've been the best at whatever he chose to do in his life.

As baseball fans, we're lucky that he chose to do what he's done so well.

TONY GWYNN JR.

"Wherever I'm around Ted, I'm always laughing because he makes me laugh."

A GRADUATE OF Poway High School, Tony Gwynn Jr., went on to play baseball at his late father's alma mater, San Diego State University.

An outfielder who was drafted by the Milwaukee Brewers in the second round of the 2003 MLB Draft, Gwynn spent eight seasons in the major leagues, including 2009 and 2010 with the Padres.

He started his Padres' broadcast career in 2017, alongside both Ted Leitner and Jesse Agler, and since 2021 has served as color analyst with Agler on the team's radio broadcasts.

From the time I was just a little kid, what I like to call the "voice in my head" about baseball was shaped by Ted Leitner.

When I grew up in the 1980s, that was back when you didn't have every game on TV and just about everyone listened to the Padres on the radio.

Ted and Jerry were the voices that told me, this is what Padres baseball is all about.

Now, wherever I'm around Ted, I'm always laughing because he makes me laugh. I'm not that hard to entertain anyway, but he makes me laugh, and I mean, always.

In a lot of ways, the relationship I've had with Ted was shaped by the close relationship my father and Ted had. When my dad was a player, they got to be very tight and their friend-ship grew even closer over the years.

With the exception of my family, Ted was as close as anyone to my dad. They really enjoyed being around each other.

MARK GRANT

"I just love Teddy dear-ly and think the world of him, always have."

MARK GRANT, WHO BEGAN his Padres broadcast career in 1997 as a color ana-lyst, has been paired since 2016 with current play-by-play voice Don Orsillo.

A former No. 1 draft choice of the San Francisco Giants (1981) as a right-handed pitcher, Grant spent nine sea-sons in the majors, including a four-year stint with the Padres (1987–1990) as one of the team's most popular players.

Noted for his humorous antics and remarks, Grant answers easily to "Mud" and "Mudcat," refer-ences to the late major-league pitcher Jim Grant whose nick-name was "Mudcat."

To me, Ted has been the way he is for as long as I've known him.

He's always been "the man," a guy whom I liked and respect-ed, and loved being around. I didn't really get to know him un-til I joined the Padres' telecasts, but right away, we made each other laugh a lot.

Now, whenever we see each other, it's the same thing, we start laughing about something one of us says and we can't stop. And nobody makes me laugh like Ted.

In past seasons, when we'd have some dead time an hour or so before the game, Don (Orsillo) and I would take a quick stroll over to the radio booth and just chat with Teddy.

Whatever he'd talk about, he'd always make us laugh, which got us in a great frame of mind to do the game.

At the beginning of the 2021 season, after I learned that he took a painful tumble outside Petco Park, I wrote him a text to see how he was doing and to wish him well.

His return text to me was, "Sidewalk 1, Leitner 0."

One of my favorite stories was when we were in Denver about four or five years ago and the guys on the team were already on the bus, headed to the airport.

Ted, who was one of the last people on-board, climbed up the steps and then stopped in the aisle to make a pronouncement: "Ahh...FYI, the green liquid in the small bottle in your bathroom is NOT mouthwash."

And we're all cracking up.

What happened was, he thought what he had picked up was a small bottle of mouthwash, so he took a quick swig before spitting it out, because it was actually shampoo.

I just love Teddy dearly and think the world of him, always have.

ALICIA GWYNN

"Ted has a voice that's like a magnet that attaches to your heart."

AN ENTREPRENEUR, BUSINESS EX-ECUTIVE and philanthropist, Alicia Gwynn is the widow of Tony Gwynn, who died at age 54 in 2014.

Mrs. Gwynn is currently president of Gwynndustries, a Poway-based enterprise that honors Tony Gwynn's memory with signature ventures based on family recipes, specialty wines, and music performed by their daughter Anisha.

She also presides over the Tony and Alicia Gwynn Foundation.

In the early 1980s, at Tony's request, Alicia began video recording each of his at-bats, which enabled him to better analyze his hitting swing. The use of video helped Tony raise his skills to new heights and soon revolutionized the game.

───※───

Ted was always in my husband's corner, going back when Tony was playing basketball for the Aztecs. Even though I didn't know him very well then, I loved hearing him talk about my husband on the radio.

When Tony was playing basketball, I'd go to the games at the Sports Arena with Mr. Gwynn, Tony's father, and he would listen to Ted on his ear buds.

He loved listening to Ted. When Tony did something exciting on the court, Ted always had a magical excitement in his voice.

Same thing when Tony was with the Padres. Listening to Ted has always been a joy for our entire family.

Through the years, Ted was always Tony's favorite. Whenever Tony saw Ted, he'd say, "Hey, Theodore, let's talk."

They'd sit together in the dugout and tell each other stories and make each other laugh. Their friendship only grew stronger over time.

Ted has a voice that's like a magnet that attaches to your heart. He takes you to that moment like there's no other moment, like you feel you have to listen.

Through all the years, I'd say what Tony and Ted sensed in each other was their shared loyalty.

Tony would often tell me, "Ted will always tell you the truth, whether you want to hear it or not," and I don't think Tony would've had it any other way.

When Ted was doing his talk show, once in a while he'd get asked by female callers if Tony was married. And Ted would say, without a moment's hesitation, "Yes, happily, to a wonderful young lady named Alicia."

That always made me feel good.

BOB CHANDLER

A LONG-TIME SAN DIEGO SPORTS-CASTER, Bob Chandler spent more than 25 seasons as a Padres' voice, handling play-by-play and color duties at various times, often paired with Ted Leitner.

A native San Diegan known for his encyclopedic knowledge and recall of local sports history, especially regarding the Padres, Chandler began his on-air career in 1961 after graduating from San Diego State University.

"We'd go out to dinner and he'd always reach for the check and pick up the tab."

Along with local baseball historian Bill Swank, Chandler is the co-author of *Bob Chandler's Tales from the San Diego Padres Dugout*, a collection of anecdotes from the Padres' formative years.

⸻

Younger Padres fans may not realize it, but when Ted first came to Channel 8 and KFMB in the late 1970s, he was like a rock star, just an absolute sensation.

I remember doing a game from Yuma at Desert Sun Stadium, and throughout the game, the fans sitting just below us treated him like he was a Hollywood celebrity, which he didn't seem to mind.

Some people may think he doesn't prepare for his broadcasts, but in the 25 years we worked together, he always came into the booth fully prepared. Maybe not in the usual way, with a prepared script or written notes, but it was all in his head.

No matter what the topic, whether it was about baseball or not, he knew exactly what he was going to say – well, maybe not the exact words. But he always knew the stories he wanted to tell and the topics he wanted to bring up during the game.

When that red light went on, Ted was on, and he's stayed "on" for as long as I've known him.

We traveled together for about 25 years and I always found Ted to be very generous. We'd go out to dinner and he'd always reach for the check and pick up the tab. He was just very fun to travel with.

To sum up my thoughts about Ted, which isn't all that easy because he's a very complex guy, let me just say that he's among the best all-around broadcasters I've ever known, maybe THE best.

And I've always valued our friendship.

RANDY JONES

"All he did was tell the truth and what's wrong with that?"

A FORMER CY YOUNG AWARD WINNER in 1976, Randy Jones ranks among the Padres' all-time most popular players.

After his eight Padres seasons (1974–1980), he later pitched for the New York Mets (1981–1982) before retiring.

Known for his sinkerball pitch, which baffled opponents for its movement and lack of velocity, Jones, who attended Chapman University, was drafted by the Padres in the fifth round of the 1972 MLB Draft.

The affable left-hander has been a Padres' radio voice since the early 1980s. His popular namesake BBQ restaurant, Randy Jones BBQ, has long been a Petco Park favorite, with his retired No. 35 displayed at the Park Avenue entrance.

───── ∞ ─────

I'll tell you this, when Ted Leitner first came to town, he sure knew how to piss off our players.

He wasn't shy about voicing his opinions about how we were playing, which usually wasn't very good. He had a gift for knowing how to stir things up, so he wasn't exactly beloved in the clubhouse, which didn't bother him one bit.

On the good side, he did light a fire under some of our guys, who, let's face it, needed it.

As for me, when I was a player, I got a kick out of him. I mean,

all he did was tell the truth and what's wrong with that? My phi-
losophy has always been, if you don't want to hear the truth about
how badly you're playing, stop complaining and play better.

With everything Ted has done for Padres baseball, his pas-
sion and love for the game, it's unprecedented.

Nobody I know loves the Padres more than Ted does, and
no one has done more to generate the fans' enthusiasm over the
years.

NICK CANEPA

KNOWN TO COLLEAGUES AS "The Godfather," Nick Canepa of *The San Diego Union Tribune* has been a popular and opinionated sportswriter-columnist for nearly 50 years.

A native San Diegan, Canepa began working for the *San Diego Evening Tribune* in 1971 as a clerk.

"I don't know how he found the time, but for a long time he was every-where and did everything."

Three years later, he joined the afternoon paper's sports staff, eventually covering San Diego State football and basketball, plus the NBA's Clippers and the NFL's Chargers.

He has been a general sports columnist since 1984.

———— ⚭ ————

I've known Ted since he got off the plane from Philadelphia in
early 1978.

At that time, I was doing a sports media column for the

afternoon paper, so I've gotten to know him well over these years.

He's had an enormous impact on this town as a ground-breaker in a lot of ways. I mean, who else did what Ted Leitner did? Nobody. There were just guys who recited scores and highlights and that's about it.

It wasn't long before he became the play-by-play voice of every team we had here, doing all his TV and radio stuff. Plus, besides his traveling with the Padres, Aztecs and Chargers, I know that he also volunteered a lot of time doing charity functions, civic events, speeches.

I swear, I don't know how he found the time, but for a long time he was everywhere and did everything.

In 1989, Ted asked me to be his color guy for the San Diego CIF high school football title game, Morse vs. Rancho Bueno Vista, led by a quarterback named Dave Roberts.

By then, I was a columnist and wasn't covering prep sports at all. And I don't think Ted had done play-by-play of any prep games until that one.

But we called that game, and it was like he was calling the Chargers. With absolutely no notes in front of him, he knew everyone on both teams. It was uncanny, like he'd done their games all season long.

Like I say, he used to be everywhere and now he's not. And that's a shame.

JIM LASLAVIC

"He's just an incredible talent, not only bright, but brilliant and so entertaining."

A FORMER NFL LINEBACKER who spent 10 years in the NFL, including four seasons with the Chargers, Jim Laslavic joined San Diego's CBS-8 in 1983 as weekend sports anchor, when Ted Leitner was the station's lead sports voice.

A proud graduate of Penn State University, the personable Laslavic is best known as "Laz."

He went on to enjoy a 30-year career as NBC-7's lead sports anchor, along with various roles as talk-show host, Chargers' radio color analyst, and host of *SportsWrap*, his Sunday night interview/highlights show.

When I first got into TV, Ted and I shared an office at Channel 8 during the six years when we worked together.

I often joked that I shared an office not with Ted, but with his desk. He was always so busy with his many commitments that he rarely came into our office.

His desk would get stacked higher and higher with bags stuffed with letters that came to him from viewers.

Finally, I said, "Ted, how 'bout I start opening some of these for you?"

I was absolutely amazed at how passionate those letters were, for and against Ted and what he was saying on the air.

I was just starting out and had so much to learn, and here he was, an absolute pro with a huge following, and he couldn't have been nicer.

Ted didn't feel that it was his job to be my hands-on teacher, per se, but he made it clear with his viewers and listeners that, hey, give this new guy a chance.

To this day, I greatly respect him for what he did for me.

He's just an incredible talent, not only bright, but brilliant and so entertaining. We're lucky in San Diego that he decided to stay.

I can't imagine this town without Ted Leitner.

RICH OHRNBERGER

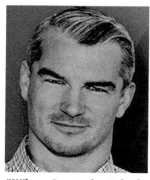

"When I got the job, he called me up and said, 'We're gonna have a lot of fun.'"

A FORMER OFFENSIVE GUARD for the San Diego Chargers (2013–2014), Rich Ohrnberger has served since 2017 as color analyst for San Diego State's football radio broadcasts alongside play-by-play voice Ted Leitner.

A graduate of Penn State who's analytical and thoughtful in his approach to the game, Ohrnberger also played for the New England Patriots and the Arizona Cardinals during his NFL career.

Two years after retiring as a player following the 2014 season, he joined the on-air lineup of XTRA-AM Radio.

—◦◦◦—

When I think of Ted Leitner, I think of one of the most conversational human beings I've ever met.

Truly, when you walk into the broadcast booth with Ted before the game even starts, your conversation with him has already been going on and you get enveloped into whatever you both happen to be talking about.

Then, when the game is over, I'll think to myself, "You're basically getting paid to have a great conversation with Ted Leitner and talk about the sport – college football – that you both love to talk about.

"And you're doing that with an extremely gifted broadcaster who's also become a great friend."

For the first Aztecs game we worked together, I must've spent months putting together what's called a "spotting board," to get to know the players and their positions.

I had assumed that all play-by-play guys and color analysts relied on spotting boards to make sure they had all the information they needed to do the game.

Except for Ted, as I was to find out.

When I first got the job, he called me up and said, "We're gonna have a lot of fun," but we didn't meet in person until just before that first game.

When I walked into the booth with my elaborate spotting boards and what I thought was my wealth of information, I was ready to knock my first Aztecs broadcast out of the park.

He looked at me and said, "How long did THAT take you?"

When I proudly told him that I'd been working on it for months, all he said was, "You won't need it," and he was right.

When we wrapped up that first game, it was like I said to myself, "What game?" We just had a running conversation about what was happening in front of us, all very relaxed and conversational, like we'd known each other for years.

That was the easiest acclimation to a new job that any broadcast partner could ever ask for. And it continues to this day.

DON ORSILLO

THE PADRES' TV PLAY-BY-PLAY VOICE on Bally Sports, Don Orsillo, came to San Diego in 2016, succeeding the late Dick Enberg after his retirement.

On the Padres' telecasts, Orsillo partners with color analysts Mark Grant and Mark Sweeney. Previously, Orsillo had spent 15 seasons as the TV voice of the Boston Red Sox (2001–2015).

His mix of play-by-play with personal storytelling is absolutely unique in our business.

A native of Massachusetts whose family moved to Southern California when he was a teenager, Orsillo was exceptionally popular with Red Sox viewers – as well as the players whose games he called for years.

───────◦◦◦◦───────

When I was in high school in Palos Verdes, for some reason our cable TV package included San Diego's Channel 8, and there was this guy Ted Leitner, who was always on.

So, even without knowing him, I became a huge Ted Leitner fan. Many years later, when I joined the Red Sox, I got to know his play-by-play by listening to his calls on MLB Radio. But I didn't really know him.

Later, when I came to the Padres in 2016, I discovered that the Ted Leitner I thought I "knew" in Palo Verdes was still the same character that I remembered. Because there's no one like Ted.

For me, his mix of play-by-play with personal storytelling is absolutely unique in our business, with the one slight exception being the Yankees' John Sterling. Their styles are similar, but different, if that makes sense.

I believe doing baseball play-by-play in a local market is not only about describing the game action, but it's about telling stories and showing your personality, like Mud and I try to do as much as possible with the Padres.

Ted has always done that. And nobody does baseball like Ted.

BOB SCANLAN

"I knew I was going to get at least one 'Leitner gem' and usually more, about something I never knew before."

AMONG THE TALLEST PITCHERS in major-league history, the 6-8 Bob Scanlan had stints with seven teams over his nine-year career, mostly as a right-handed relief pitcher.

A fluent Spanish-speaker, Scanlan also played for five seasons in the Dominican Republic, Venezuela, and Mexico.

Scanlan joined the Padres' broadcast team in 2004, where he has served in various roles including sideline reporter, radio color analyst with Ted Leitner, and periodic play-by-play voice.

When I think of Ted Leitner, I think "broadcast genius."

Because that's what he is.

For me, to be excellent in one sport is incredible in itself, but to be as excellent as Ted is in baseball, football and basketball has always amazed me.

It's not just his adaptability and his versatility that was so impressive. It was his ability to recall so many stories and weave them into the flow of the game.

What he told his listeners wasn't just the cursory information that you'd see on a stat sheet or read in a game program, which he knew because of his amazing photographic memory and instant recall.

But he would always tell the right story at the right time, without missing a pitch or a play.

Not only that, but he had this uncanny ability to tap into all the different facets of his own life, because he's had so many different experiences and been around so many fascinating people.

When I was working with him, I'd be just as fascinated as his listeners, happy to be along for the ride on this magical journey we were sharing.

All the while, you'd still be enthralled in the game itself because no matter what story he was telling, he'd always bring you back to the play-by-play.

When I came to the ballpark – and it was an honor to be his color analyst for four years – I knew I was going to get at least one 'Leitner gem' and usually more, about something I never knew before.

I was grateful for that, every single day.

TREVOR HOFFMAN

TREVOR HOFFMAN WAS ACQUIRED by the Padres in mid-1993 in a multi-player trade that sent the Padres' Gary Sheffield to the Miami Marlins.

Over his next 16 years with the Padres, Hoffman was to emerge as major-league baseball's all-time saves leader, whose late-inning entrance into home games was heralded by AC/DC's foreboding "Hell's Bells," which became his entry anthem.

"I have so much respect for him, just as I had for Jerry Coleman."

The personable Hoffman was inducted into baseball's Hall of Fame in 2014, and has since served in various Padres' front-office and instructor roles.

———∞———

When I first came to the Padres in 1997, let's just say that I noticed that Ted was the biggest media dude in town and that he said what he thought.

He wasn't exactly a beloved figure in our clubhouse, because it seemed like every time we saw him on TV, he'd talk crap about us. We'd say, "How does this guy have that much power to rip us all the time?"

Of course, we weren't aware of how much knowledge he had about sports in general, and baseball in particular, and how much he loved the game.

I have to say that in the past 20 years or so, I've gotten to know Ted a lot better and I always get a kick out of being around him.

I have so much respect for him, just as I had for Jerry Cole-man. And I've come to respect his storytelling and his reverence for the game and its history.

LARRY LUCCHINO

"I've often said that Ted Leitner is an acquired taste and I acquired it fairly early."

THE DRIVING FORCE BEHIND Petco Park, Larry Lucchino was the Padres' president/CEO for seven seasons (1995-2001), and is regarded among the most astute and effective top executives in MLB history.

After he left the Padres, he spent 14 years in the same leadership role with the Boston Red Sox, modernizing Fenway Park and overseeing the rebuilding of that storied franchise from top to bottom.

During that span, the BoSox won four World Series titles.

Lucchino was a starting guard and teammate of the legendary Bill Bradley at Princeton, which reached the Final Four of the 1965 NCAA Tournament.

When I was there, Ted Leitner was not just the Padres' broadcaster, he was part of the essential fabric of San Diego, a colorful and often controversial slice of home-cooking.

His versatility and sense of self-deprecation made him a

constant topic of conversation among our fans and supporters, which was one of his many strengths.

One of the things I admired most about him was the respect and deference he showed Jerry Coleman when they were doing our games together. Ted was second to no one in his genuine love and respect for Jerry, who was a beloved figure to our fans, as was Ted, but in a different way, of course.

I've often said that Ted Leitner is an acquired taste and I acquired it fairly early in what became our long friendship. Because when you really get to know Ted, when you get beyond the blarney and bluster, you'll find a very thoughtful, caring and reflective person.

I've been gone from San Diego for about 25 years now, but if I were trying to get my finger on the pulse of the city again, I would first go to Ted Leitner.

STEVE FISHER

"I went up to him during a break and asked if he'd like to give our team a little pep talk."

THE GENIAL COACH KNOWN simply as "Fish" led San Diego State University to eight NCAA Tournament berths, and was honored with two national Coach of the Year awards.

His 18-year reign coincided with that of Ted Leitner as the Aztecs' play-by-play voice.

The Aztecs' all-time winningest coach, Fisher retired at the end of the 2016–2017 season, succeeded by Brian Dutcher, his longtime assistant coach at Michigan and SDSU.

With his patient approach to players and media, Fisher crafted a program that now ranks among the nation's most respected.

The Fisher era not only brought on-court dominance, but a regular succession of 12,500-plus sellouts to Viejas Arena, the Aztecs' on-campus arena. In his honor, the playing surface is named Steve Fisher Court.

When I came to town in 1999, it very quickly became apparent to me that this Ted Leitner was something special, extraordinary even.

He was everywhere, doing everything.

One day, early in the 2010–2011 season, when we had Kawhi (Leonard) and Malcolm Thomas, the group that went

34-3, I went up to him during a break and asked if he'd like to give our team a little pep talk.

He said, absolutely, and it was clear he was thrilled to be asked.

After practice, we all gathered together and Ted talked to the guys for about 15 minutes about how he thought this was a special group that could accomplish a lot.

At one point, he asked the players to close their eyes and to dream about what their futures might hold, not only for this season, but for the rest of their lives.

When he was about to wrap it up, he said, "Now, I have one more thing to tell you. This is the most important thing that you'll ever hear. I wish that I had learned it sooner. You don't learn it in college and you're not going to get it on the basketball court.

"But it's something that could be monumental in terms of your life moving forward."

We all moved closer to him, eager to hear what he was going to say next.

"One word: Prenuptial."

I cracked a smile, but I could tell that my players didn't know what to do. They looked at me, then looked at Ted and he started laughing, like only Ted Leitner laughs. And then everyone was laughing as they gave him a standing ovation.

That was Ted being Ted, and I'm proud to call him my friend.

JOE BAUER

FOR MORE THAN 23 YEARS (1975–1997), Joe Bauer was half of KFMB Radio's hugely successful morning-drive radio team of Hudson & Bauer, which featured two lengthy segments daily with Ted Leitner.

Along with H&B and airing the Padres' games, KFMB was the Tiffany's of local radio, both in ratings and revenues

No longer in broadcasting, Bauer is now semi-retired and resides in Salt

"Sometimes, we'd be laughing so hard that we'd completely forget we were on the air."

Lake City.

⸺⁂⸺

Whenever Mac and I MC'ed charity events around town, our listeners would come up and ask about Ted, wanting to know what he was really like. I'd tell people that what you heard on our show was what you got with Ted.

He didn't socialize all that much, but when he got in front of a microphone, that was Ted. His segments gave our listeners an opportunity to hear a whole different side to him, apart from his Channel 8 sports stuff. And there was no one like Ted.

For Mac and me, being on with Ted was like hanging out with your buddies, goofing around, telling stories. Sometimes, we'd be laughing so hard that we'd completely forget we were on the air.

What I remember most is that we were having so much fun

that I couldn't wait to go to bed at night, so I could come into the studio early the next morning.

Ted was a very big, big part of our success.

MATT VASGERSIAN

ONE OF BASEBALL'S MOST VERSATILE and admired play-by-play voices, Matt Vasgersian served as the Padres' lead TV voice from 2002 to 2008, teamed with color analyst Mark Grant.

Now with MLB Network as its lead voice and studio host, Vasgersian also does play-by-play for the Los Angeles Angels.

The former voice of the Milwaukee Brewers (1997–2001), he has handled play-by-play for Fox Sports' NFL coverage, the Olympics, college bowl games, USC men's basketball, Ultimate Fighting Championship bouts, and the short-lived XFL.

"Someone in my broadcast crew said, 'That's Ted Leitner. He does everything in this town.'"

There are plenty of people in this business who think they're original, and in fact, we're just about all derivative of someone else's style. But I can't say that about Ted, because he's always been an original.

The first time I saw Ted, I was doing the Brewers' games in the late 1990s and we were at Qualcomm Stadium. I'd always heard about this guy named Leitner. And this was when he was at his peak of his powers.

I recall seeing him scurry into the press box, with only 30 minutes, probably less, before game-time and he's wearing a coat and tie because he's just wrapped up his 6 o'clock segment on Channel 8.

---

*Someone on my broadcast crew said,
"That's Ted Leitner. He does everything in this town."*

Well, now I'm the one who's trying to do everything I can in this business. Ted was one of the guys who made it work – doing the things that play-by-play guys like us like to do, but he did everything at the same time, which just amazed me.

When I think of Ted, I can't help but think of that local spot for DZ Akin's Delicatessen that ran on local TV. Ted's sitting alone in a booth, waiting for the server to bring his order. When it arrives, he's making a referee's field goal signal and then declaring, "SCOOORRRE!"

I can't tell you how many times Mark Grant and I would be having a meal and the food would arrive and we'd shout out in unison, "SCOOORRRE!"

On a personal level, I admire the guy and his talent so very much.

TIM FLANNERY

ONE OF THE MOST POPULAR PLAYERS in Padres' history, Tim Flannery has a long history with the team.

His career spanned 11 seasons (1979–1989) as a utility infielder-second baseman with hustle and flair, then as the team's third-base coach (1996–2002) under then-manager Bruce Bochy.

"He'd make that moment shine, no matter what was going on in his personal life."

During the Padres' 2004–2006 seasons, Flannery served as Ted Leitner's color analyst.

Following the 2006 season, he was reunited with Bochy, who hired him after both had left the Padres.

───※───

Ted was a great teacher for me, which I really appreciated, because doing radio, especially play-by-play, can be pretty painful if you don't know what you're doing. Ted helped me get through that learning process.

There's no other way to learn to do play-by-play, except to do it, and he's the guy who encouraged me to give it a try.

What I always respected about Ted is the same thing that I respect about the best ballplayers, as well as my fellow musicians, was his ability to be at the top of his game when he turned on that mic.

It always amazed me that after I'd finished giving the starting lineups and handed the mic over to him, he'd make that moment shine, no matter what was going on in his personal life.

When it's time to perform, when that red light goes on, or when you take the stage, whatever, I know how tough it is to give your best – every night.

Ted always did.

BRUCE BOCHY

"I've always admired Ted, enjoyed being with him, enjoyed laughing with him, going way back when I was with the Padres."

A FORMER PADRES CATCHER for five seasons (1983–1987) and later, the team's highly regarded manager for 12 years (1995–2006), Bruce Bochy rose to greater fame as manager of the San Francisco Giants (2007–2019).

During that span, he led the Giants to World Series wins in 2010, 2012 and 2014, the lasting legacy of his 25-year managerial career.

In 1984, he was the Padres' back-up catcher when the Padres reached the World Series, and he served as manager when the Padres reached the post-season playoffs in 1996, 1998 (World Series), 2005, and 2006.

Bochy retired from the Giants following the 2019 season.

First of all, I've always admired Ted, enjoyed being with him,

enjoyed laughing with him, going way back when I was with the Padres.

He's such a great entertainer and storyteller, and not just when he's doing games, whether it's baseball or basketball or football, but whenever we happen to see each other. He's always got new stories to tell.

Over the years, we've been speakers at so many events together where he's the absolute star of the show. He'll get everybody laughing hysterically like he was a standup comedian, as funny as any of 'em.

I know this much, he does a great job doing baseball, but he's not into analytics and all that stuff. He's more into telling stories, on and off the air, and it was always fun to catch up when we'd see each other around the batting cage.

He knows the game of baseball, that's for sure. Shoot, I've always thought the world of Ted.

KEN LEVINE

A HIGHLY RESPECTED TV COM-EDY producer and scriptwriter, Ken Levine has sitcom credits that include *M*A*S*H*, *The Simpsons*, *Frasier*, *Everybody Loves Raymond* and others.

He's also an avid baseball fan, so much so that he served alongside Jerry Coleman and Ted Leitner for two seasons (1995–1996) as a Padres' play-by-play voice, a role he's also had with the Baltimore Orioles and Seattle Mariners.

"When you listen to Ted, you get the feeling that he's talking only to you, one-on-one."

When I was sharing the booth with Ted and Jerry, I'd be amazed at Ted's work commitments beyond just doing the Padres.

We'd be in Montreal or Philadelphia or wherever after doing a night game and we'd have a flight the next morning, wherever we were going.

While Jerry and I were trying to catch up on some much-needed sleep, Ted would be setting up his audio equipment at 4 o'clock in the morning in his hotel room, getting ready for his morning-show bits with Hudson & Bauer.

He always seemed unruffled by his schedule, but I would just be a wreck if I tried to keep up with him.

There's another thing about Ted that I really appreciated and have tried to emulate. He is an absolutely terrific on-air salesman. His commercials are like Paul Harvey's used to be from a different era.

Ted is so convincing because he talks directly to his listeners, which is just one of his many strengths. When you listen to Ted, you get the feeling that he's talking only to you, one-on-one.

For me, it was so much fun working with Ted because many times I'd have no idea what he was going to talk about next. The same thing held true with his listeners, I'm sure, which was part of his appeal.

He's such a gifted story-teller, and it didn't matter whether the Padres were winning or losing. A lot of his listeners probably wanted to just relax with a beer and listen to what Ted had to say that night.

Often, that was better than the game itself.

When you're doing the games of a bad team, and there have been quite a few bad Padres teams over the years, let's say they're down 7–1 in the 4th inning, why would anyone want to listen?

Well, you wanted to listen because of Ted.

MARK SWEENEY

A THREE-TIME MEMBER OF THE PA-
DRES as a player (1997–1998, 2002,
2005), Mark Sweeney spent 13 seasons in the major leagues, for a total
of seven MLB teams.

Sweeney was best known for his
timely pinch-hitting, a category in
which he ranks second all-time for
pinch hits with 175.

The versatile Sweeney serves as the
Padres' TV host with Mike Pomeranz,
along with periodic roles as a TV/radio analyst.

"Ted was one of those guys you loved to see at the ballpark every day."

*For me, Ted Leitner will always be synonymous with Padres
baseball, just like Jerry Coleman.*

*When I played for the Padres, I'd come out for BP and Ted
would be sitting in the dugout with Tony Gwynn, laughing and
having a great time. We regarded Ted was one of those guys you
loved to see at the ballpark every day.*

*For me, because I was close friends with Trevor Hoffman,
having Ted host the Petco Park salute to Trevor's Hall of
Fame induction was the perfect matchup of people I liked and
respected.*

*Ted knocked it out of the park and the ceremony turned out
to be spectacular, which Trevor deserved but would never ask
for.*

Of course, Ted reached the same heights in his tributes to

Jerry Coleman and Tony Gwynn, both of whom loved the Padres as much as Ted does.

I think the world of Teddy and I miss him. I know this: He'll always be a big part of Padres baseball.

VIN SCULLY

REGARDED AS THE PREEMINENT baseball announcer of all time, Vin Scully spent 67 years (1950–2016) as the play-by-play voice of the Dodgers, going back to their days in Brooklyn and continuing in Los Angeles.

With his eloquent speech, precise diction and impeccable story-telling, Scully was known for this invitation to his legions of listeners, "Pull up a chair and spend part of Sunday with us."

His Dodgers' career stands as the longest tenure of any broadcaster with one team in the history of professional sports.

"Doing 41 years at the same job, calling baseball games, is not only arduous and difficult, it's also a tribute to the man himself."

⸻

I know this about Ted Leitner: He has pleased his listeners by being accurate, informative and entertaining for a very long time, which is not that easy to do.

What I can tell you is that doing 41 years at the same job, calling baseball games, is not only arduous and difficult, it's also a tribute to the man himself.

For being such a popular fixture in San Diego for so many years, he has my utmost admiration and respect. If you could be so kind, please pass along my best wishes and congratulations to Ted.

RALPH LAWLER

THE LONGTIME VOICE of the NBA's Los Angeles Clippers, Ralph Lawler handled radio play-by-play for much of the six seasons (1978–1984) that the franchise was based in San Diego.

Prior to coming to San Diego, Lawler had briefly succeeded Leitner as the TV sports anchor at Philadelphia's WCAU.

"Everybody was really excited about this 'new guy' who was coming in."

Over the span of his 40-year career, which ended with his retirement following the 2018–2019 season, Lawler missed only three Clippers games.

⸺⸎⸺

Back in the late 1970s, I was working in Philadelphia at WCAU Radio and when Tom Brookshier, who was the nightly TV sports guy, left for CBS Sports, that created a big opening.

Ted had been a sensation in Hartford, so they brought him in as the nightly TV sports guy on our 5, 6, and 11 newscasts.

That's when they brought me over from the radio side to be the weekend sports guy and feature sports reporter.

Everybody was really excited about this "new guy" who was coming in, and Ted had a very unique style.

Most guys in our business try to fit into the cookie-cutter mold of what a broadcaster is supposed to sound like, how he's supposed to act, what he's supposed to talk about.

But that's not Ted.

Before he got to Philadelphia, he threw that mold away. He'd go on the air without a script, with a list of five or six stories he wanted to cover, and he drove his producers and directors positively nuts, trying to follow him.

Ted treated sports like it was the funny pages of the news cycle, but people in Philadelphia regarded sports as a religious experience.

To them, if you talked about the Phillies or the Flyers or the Eagles or the 76ers, you'd better be serious. But Ted had a light-hearted approach and it just didn't work.

When WCAU let Ted go, they replaced him with me. Then, of course, Ted came out to San Diego, where his style was much better accepted, and I joined him a short time later.

I've always had great admiration for Ted because he dared to be different, which takes a lot of courage in our business.

JOHN MOORES

"Ted said, 'Did I ever marry anybody? I married everybody!'"

The Padres' owner from 1994 until 2009, John Moores partnered with president/CEO Larry Lucchino in upgrading the franchise, on and off the field, led by the opening of Petco Park in 2004.

A Houston-based software engineer and entrepreneur, Moores purchased the Padres from TV executive Tom Werner for a reported $94 million.

Moores later sold the Padres for a reported $800 million to a group headed by San Diego's Ron Fowler in 2012, including brothers Peter and Tom Seidler, grandsons of legendary Dodgers owner Walter O'Malley.

Throughout his time in San Diego, Moores has been a generous donor to San Diego State University and UC San Diego, along with his ongoing support of numerous civic, cultural and charitable causes.

———— ∞ ————

I first met Ted in early 1995 after I bought the Padres.

Before coming to San Diego, I'd been in Houston, so I'd never seen him on TV and didn't know anything about him.

When I told him that, he said, "You mean, you've never seen me on TV before?"

I looked at him and said, "Nope."

He laughed, and so did I, but that must've been very unusual for Ted because everybody knew who he was back then.

Ted and I share a birthday, and every year we don't just say "Happy birthday" to each other, we remind ourselves that we also share the day with Tom Hanks, and God help us, O.J. Simpson.

When you think about it, I'd bet that more San Diegans, at least those of a certain age, have heard Ted Leitner's voice more in their lifetime than they heard their own mother's.

When I was about to get married a second time, I asked Ted if he'd ever married anybody.

Stunned that I would ask that question, he said, "Did I ever marry anybody? I married everybody!"

What I meant, of course, was that I was hoping he would agree to officiate at my wedding. He graciously accepted and was absolutely brilliant.

I always thought that Ted worked too hard. He had a studio in his house and did all those games, plus his TV work and talk show and all those commercials.

He did those radio voice-over commercials for D.Z. Akin's and all the others, always without a script and usually on one take, timed exactly within 30 seconds or 60 seconds. That was amazing to me.

One day, I asked him how he knew exactly how long he should talk, all without using a stopwatch or a script.

And he said, "I just know."

With all due respect to my dear friend, I know that he doesn't give himself enough credit for how brilliant he has been.

TED LEITNER

Controversial, outrageous and hilarious, Ted Leitner has been the enduring voice of San Diego's sports scene since 1978.

As of 2021, Leitner spent 41 seasons as the play-by-play voice of the San Diego Padres and 25 years as the radio voice of football and basketball for the San Diego State University Aztecs.

During that span, he also spent 25 years (1978–2002) as sports anchor and commentator on CBS 8 and talk-show host and sports humorist on KFMB-AM Radio.

Prior to coming to San Diego in 1978, Leitner was a TV sports personality in Oklahoma City, Hartford, and Philadelphia.

In addition to the Padres and Aztecs, his play-by-play credits include the NFL's San Diego Chargers and Philadelphia Eagles, the NBA's San Diego Clippers, as well as the University of Oklahoma and the University of Connecticut.

A native of New York, he earned a TV/Radio/Film degree at Oklahoma State University and a master's degree from the University of Oklahoma.

Long a familiar fixture in San Diego, he has MC'ed thousands of events, led by the Padres' annual Opening Day ceremonies, the team's Hall of Fame induction ceremonies, and "Jerry Coleman Day" in 2012, paying tribute to his longtime broadcast partner.

Notably, he also served as MC for the Petco Park memorial services devoted to Coleman (January 5, 2014) and later that year, for Tony Gwynn (June 16, 2014).

On January 15, 2021, Leitner was officially appointed Padres Ambassador by team owner and chairman, Peter Seidler.

Leitner has six sons: twins Nick and Ryan, Mark, Matthew, Jordan and Teddy; a daughter, Kristin; a grandson, Adam; and three granddaughters, Scarlett, Cecily and Sofia.

JOHN FREEMAN

An author and PR professional, John Freeman is a former media columnist and sportswriter with the *San Diego Union-Tribune.*

In recent years, he has written a series of legacy books with notable San Diegans, told in a first-person narrative format.

Earlier in his career, he served as New York-based staff editor/writer with the Yankees and later, publications director with the NBA.

In 2014, he collaborated on *They Called Me God* (Simon & Schuster), a first-person book with Hall of Fame baseball umpire Doug Harvey.

A graduate of the University of Arizona, John is based in San Diego.

He proudly dedicates *TED TALKS* to his son James and daughter Elizabeth.